PENTAGON PRESS

COMMITTED TO SERVE THE ARMED FORCES

INDIA AND CHINA

National Image-building in Southeast Asia

INDIA AND CHINA

National Image-building in Southeast Asia

Parama Sinha Palit

MAULANA ABUL KALAM AZAD INSTITUTE OF ASIAN STUDIES
KOLKATA

PENTAGON PRESS

India and China: National Image-building in Southeast Asia
By Parama Sinha Palit

ISBN 978-93-86618-26-9

First Published in 2018

Published by
PENTAGON PRESS
206, Peacock Lane, Shahpur Jat
New Delhi-110049
Phones: 011-64706243, 26491568
Telefax: 011-26490600
email: rajan@pentagonpress.in
website: www.pentagonpress.in

Printed at Avantika Printers Private Limited.

Contents

Acknowledgement

I take this opportunity to thank Maulana Abul Kalam Azad Institute of Asian Studies (MAKAIAS), Kolkata, and its Director Dr Sreeradha Dutta for commissioning this project to me. I have benefited from the comments of the anonymous reviewer/s who have contributed significantly in enhancing its quality and fine tuning the Manuscript for converting it into a book. I also thank experts and scholars from China, Singapore and India whom I interviewed. The book also would not have been possible without the interactions and discussions that I have had with several people along the way. I take this opportunity to deeply thank all of them for contributing to this book in various capacities and apologize for my inability to pen down many of them. Thanks also to Mr Rajan Arya and the Pentagon Press for their patient efforts in publishing this manuscript.

I also thank the Institute of Southeast Asian Studies (ISEAS) and the East Asia Institute (EAI) libraries in Singapore for their resources which I have consulted from time to time during the course of my research.

Last but not the least, I thank my family for supporting me and bearing with me all through. All errors and shortcomings, however, are entirely mine.

List of Tables

Abbreviations

ADB	Asian Development Bank
ADMM+	ASEAN Defence Ministers' Meeting Plus
AEC	ASEAN Economic Community
AEP	Act East Policy
AIIB	Asian Infrastructure Investment Bank
AMS	ASEAN Member States
APEC	Asia-Pacific Economic Cooperation
ARF	ASEAN Regional Forum
ASCC	ASEAN Socio-Cultural Community
ASEAN	Association of Southeast Asian Nations
ASEAN CBTP	ASEAN Framework Agreement on the Facilitation of Cross-Border Transport of Passengers by Road Vehicles
ASEM	Asia-Europe Meeting
BIMSTEC	Bay of Bengal Initiative for Multi-Sectoral Technical and Economic Cooperation
BJP	Bharatiya Janata Party
BRI	Belt and Road Initiative
CBMs	confidence-building-measures
CCIEE	China Centre for International Economic Exchanges
CCP	Chinese Communist Party
CD	Cultural Diplomacy

CEP	Cultural Exchange Programme
CICA	Conference on Interaction and Confidence Building in Asia
CLMV	Cambodia, Laos, Myanmar, Vietnam
COC	Code of Conduct
CPC	Communist Party of China
DPA	Development Administration Partnership
EAMF	Expanded ASEAN Maritime Forum
EAS	East Asia Summit
EEP	Education Exchange Programme
FDI	Foreign Direct Investment
FTA	Free Trade Area
GMS	Greater Mekong Sub-region
ICCR	Indian Council for Cultural Relations
IONS	Indian Ocean Naval Symposium
IOR	Indian Ocean Region
IORA	Indian Ocean Rim Association
ITE	Institute of Technical Education
ITEC	Indian Technical and Economic Cooperation
KMTTP	Kaldan Multimodal Transit Transport Project
LEP	Look East Policy
LoC	Line of Control
LOC	Line of Credit
MDB	Multilateral Development Bank
MEA	Ministry of External Affairs (Government of India)
MGC	Mekong Ganga Cooperation
MIEC	Mekong-India Economic Corridor
NATO	North Atlantic Treaty Organization
NDA	National Democratic Alliance (India)
NDRC	National Development Reform Commission (China)
NPC	National People's Congress
OBOR	One Belt One Road

OECD	Organization for Economic Co-operation and Development
PFMs	Prospective Founding Members
PM	Prime Minister
QDR	Quadrennial Defense Review
RCEP	Regional Comprehensive Economic Partnership
RVCs	Regional Value Chains
SCO	Shanghai Cooperation Organization
SLOC	Sea Lanes of Communication
SPV	Special Purpose Vehicle
TAC	Treaty of Amity and Cooperation
TPP	Trans-Pacific Partnership
UNESCAP	United Nations Economic and Social Commission for Asia and the Pacific
WEF	World Economic Forum

1

Introduction

Norman Angell, English author and journalist, noted for his work *The Great Illusion* (1910), believed wars among nation states were futile and conquests never paid. He argued against arms build-up and naval competition, which, according to him, would take nations closer to war rather than ensure peace. Agreeing with him, Australian author JDB Miller mentioned "*The Great Illusion* was that nations gained by armed confrontation, militarism, war, or conquest".[1] Soon after the publication of *The Great Illusion* in 1910, the world witnessed the First World War in 1914 that lasted for four years and was unprecedented in the slaughter, carnage and destruction that it caused. The world has witnessed more full-scale wars ever since.

Though countries now and then resolve that wars would be the "last resort", military interventions cannot be wished away altogether. This is evident from China – notwithstanding its repeated emphasis on peaceful and harmonious co-existence for assuring the world about its benign rise – pompously celebrating the seventieth anniversary of its victory over Japan on 3 September 2015. The parade, also keen to showcase China's strength, displayed its war machinery first time for its general public. This is a reminder that wars are not easily forgotten and that their outcomes continue to dictate foreign policies and shape human minds as Chinese President Xi Jinping mentioned: "War is the sword of Damocles that still hangs over mankind".[2] The three months stand off between India and China at the Doklam in the Himalayas in

2017, and India's strong stand on the issue also reflects the fragility of the current peace that otherwise seems to be in place between the two neighbours.[3]

Power and wars go hand in hand and Machiavelli's *Prince*, a treatise on wars and military force, has dictated the conduct of international affairs from the early-1500s to the Second World War (1939-45). The Peloponnesian War in the 5th century BC was partly caused by Athens' growing power that made the Spartans fearful,[4] and was marked for its naked show of power. In the *Melian Dialogue*, the Greek historian Thucydides wrote that in interstate relationships "the strong do what they have the power to do and the weak accept what they have to accept", highlighting the role of power in ancient history and its use for instilling fear in others, particularly the weaker. Kautilya's (c. 350-275 BCE) celebrated *Arthashastra* describes the absolute power of the king. Often called the Indian Machiavelli, Kautliya (also called Chanakya) didn't hesitate to support deceit and trickery for gaining and holding on to power. In later years, Clausewitz (1780-1831), a military strategist and a Prussian general, known for his unfinished work *On War*, considered war an instrument of policy and politics. Though countries have by and large avoided global wars since 1945, these have never really disappeared but have been fought in different scales and intensities in various parts of the world from time to time – the Korean War (1950-53), the Vietnam War (1956-75), the Sino-Indian War (1962), the Bangladesh Liberation War (1971), the Iran-Iraq War (1980-88), and many others. Military force continues to be exercised extensively and the world is far from being "peaceful" with traditional and non-traditional challenges and actors threatening peace and stability in the 21st century.

History also points to the difficulties encountered by countries in achieving peace. While the Peace of Nicias signed in March 421 BC between Athens and Sparta was unable to usher in peace in the Greek city states, the Treaty of Westphalia signed in October 1648, marking the end of the 30 years war, was unable to restore peace in Europe. Power instead has formed the base of realpolitik, largely concerned with achievement, exercise, maintenance, distribution and sharing of power, with countries constantly striving for peace. Political scientists like Wiseman argue that power is nothing but politics: "power is the ability to get one's wishes carried out despite opposition". This resonates well with Thucydides analysis of power of the Peloponnesian War. The great salience of political power has been forcefully emphasised by philosophers like Hobbes, one of the early power theorists in the history of Western political thought.[5] Power continues to be debated and discussed across the modern world in various contexts, sending a harsh reminder on its relevance. But as new threats and challenges confronting the state replace ancient expansionist policies of kings and emperors, the role and character of states has also transformed for adapting to the new challenges, as have policies. The modern state is not only concerned with survival like its ancient counterpart but also attempts to provide services to its citizens by attempting to become a "welfare state".

The evolution of the state has led to its role extending to social protection with the economic well being of its people as a fundamental objective of the government. As people survived wars and recovered from their aftermath, the sombre realisation that wars helped none and only depleted resources that could have been deployed in development of people began dawning upon governments. Attentions of states began shifting towards the economic well being of their people and economic development became a state priority with prosperous developed countries gaining greater international respect for their achievements and others looking forward to similar achievements. Leaderships across the world began realising that economic success was the key to global preeminence as well as domestic development. But economic progress and sustained development necessitate peace. President Xi's assertion during the same celebration in September 2015 that "We must learn the lessons of history and dedicate ourselves to peace" underlines the salience of peace in the contemporary world order. Similarly the Indian Prime Minister Modi's emphasis on world peace during one of his addresses aimed for the domestic audience through the All India Radio which he hosts every month, indicates the government's reliance on peace and harmony as domestic and foreign policy priorities. A government that has come to power promising economic development for its people, communicating such an image is significant. His assertion that "India, as a messenger of peace, has always vouched for peace, unity and harmony in the world. It is our belief that everyone should live in peace and harmony and move towards a better and peaceful tomorrow"[6] highlights the current government's interest to project an image that would perhaps assist the country's economic development.

The imperatives of peace and stability have emerged state priorities leading to an emphasis on "soft power" that has begun gaining traction in international relations. While ancient political realists like Hans. J Morgenthau, Thomas Hobbes, Spinoza and Jean-Jacques Rousseau had stated that power was the primary end of any political action, later political scientists like the British realist EH Carr have also emphasised the power over opinion, thus implying that opinions mattered. Another noted English philosopher, John Stuart Mill's submission that "the only way in which a human being can make some approach to knowing the whole of a subject, is by hearing what can be said about it by persons of every variety of opinion"[7] highlights once again the respect for the "other" opinion and accommodation of the "other". Modern American scholars like Francis Beer and Robert Hariman have argued further that "realists believe that realism is the only story of world politics...it provides neither the only plausible explanation nor the only possible world".[8]

The role of the modern state has expanded. Apart from the economic development of its people, it also aims to increase the country's stature and reputation, for which building national reputation becomes important. The imperatives have led to the rise of a group of scholars working on nation-branding, a concept analysing national efforts for improving reputation "as the image and reputation of a nation can dramatically influence its success in attracting tourism receipts and investment capital, in exports, in attracting a talented and creative workforce, and in its cultural and political influence in the world".[9] Several scholars of nation-branding define national reputation as "a collective judgment based on impressions of a variety of factors including foreign policy, responsible government, people and culture, tourism, economic strength, and brands, products, and exports".[10] Exchange of ideas, values and intercultural communication between countries have become significant in international relations with wars and military build-ups becoming more expensive and avoidable. The constructivist argument[11] – "the study of international relations must focus on the ideas and beliefs that inform the actors on the international scene as well as the shared understanding between them" – reflects the global leadership's new emphasis on cooperation and collaboration along with exchange of ideas and people to bridge borders. Realists though argue to the contrary and maintain that wars will never become obsolete even with the economic engagement intensifying or else Britain and Germany, the largest trading partners of each other, would not have fought each other in 1914.[12]

Image-Building Process and Soft Power

While striking partnerships with other countries has become an important global agenda for nation states, communicating a positive image has become an equally important long-term goal. But such an endeavour is not an entirely new concept. A positive image was regarded necessary even during the ancient times when emperors and kings were eager to impress neighbours. The Greeks' *paideia* – a system of broad cultural education – set the tone of a kind of diplomacy in which humility, modesty and respect for others were the key ideas[13] to be communicated in the conduct of interstate relations. In fact, when the Greek power was on the decline, renowned intellectuals were sent abroad as ambassadors for cultivating goodwill overseas. Identical efforts by modern states continue till date with state initiatives directed at achieving a positive image for global consumption.

Various initiatives employed by countries for communicating a positive image to the world include cultural initiatives, public diplomacy, development aid, humanitarian assistance and education. New initiatives are continuously being explored and employed for facilitating intercultural communication between states. Improving global and regional perceptions enable country leaderships to mobilise international support for their policies along with cultivating a benign external environment. The modern discourse in international relations is increasingly focusing on the advantages of pursuing soft power – a strategy that negates coercion and focuses on "softer" aspects of national power – for communicating with the international audience and strengthening engagement. While widely popular in the Western foreign policymaking for several years, soft power has gained traction in Asia and is acquiring an Asian flavour with countries like India and China becoming more image-conscious. While soft power figures prominently in China's diplomatic narrative, India is gradually co-opting the idea given New Delhi's eagerness to cultivate a positive image in line with its larger global objectives.

Both India and China have known soft power since the ancient times and have been employing them through realpolitik for advancing national interests. Both countries, apart from engaging others through cultural and public diplomacies, are also playing important roles in extending development aid and supporting the building of infrastructure and exploring new "soft" strategies for greater cooperation. International and regional forums like the World Economic Forum (WEF), Association of Southeast Asian Nations (ASEAN), Shanghai Cooperation Organisation (SCO) and many others are being employed by the leaderships for cooperating and partnering with each other for mutual benefits in an interconnected world where developments in one part impact proceedings elsewhere. However, comparing India and China's soft power approaches and applications might be too simplistic given their distinct histories and different characteristics of the states, institutions and non-state actors.[14]

Image-building is a necessity for emerging powers like India and China for facilitating their big-power role in global politics. In this respect, it is critical for "targeted" messages to reach intended audiences for obtaining desired results. Indeed, result-oriented communication for image-building has become an important focus in strategic policies. Leaderships, conscious of building images, are keen on communicating their intentions to the world audience for informing and influencing perceptions. James P. Farewell defines strategic communication "as the use of words, actions, images, or symbols to influence the attitudes and opinions of target audiences to shape their behaviour in order to advance interests or policies, or to achieve objectives".[15]

Effective communication is not new in international relations and goes back to the ancient Roman Empire that successfully communicated Rome's representation of peace, good governance and rule of law, while depicting its enemies "as barbaric, lawless and dangerous".[16] Positive image makeover entails effective communication, specifically communicating the right messages, making the words chosen and used very significant for strategic communication.[17] According to Farewell, "the language in which ideas are expressed is critical to defining a cause or strategy, and sets forth the story, plot, and narrative that underlies a strategy as well as its themes and messages".[18] The power of language, undeniably, has the ability to change perceptions. Depending on employment, language and words can arouse passion, incite, misinform, or promote constructive debates and dialogues. Thus, effective communication is the key to moulding impressions for contributing to image-building for achieving state objectives ranging from economic development of the people to being a responsible and constructive power with positive intentions. Soft power is therefore in many respects indispensable for leaderships. This makes it particularly interesting to study the policy-statements of the Indian and Chinese leaders' on their state visits to different countries and the "right noises" they make for showcasing their government's actions for impressing audiences and agencies in the countries they visit.

Coming back to soft power, its currency in modern strategic discourse is largely attributable to Joseph Nye Jr., who developed the concept in his seminal works *Bound to Lead: The Changing Nature of American Power* (1990) and *The Paradox of American Power* (2001). Nye further provided a structured conceptual paradigm of soft power in *Soft Power: The Means to Success* (2004). According to Nye, soft power is the ability of a country to persuade others to do what it wants without force or coercion. It helps shape preferences of others through appeal and attraction. This "soft" persuasion has been widely invoked in foreign policy debates of many countries including India and China and has shaped their long-term attitudes and preferences. Kurlantzick, an American contemporary journalist, looks at it more expansively: "In the context of Asia today, both China and its neighbours enunciate a broader idea of soft power, the idea that soft power implies all elements outside of the security realm, including investment and aid".[19]

Kurlantzick even cautions that China's use of soft power "is to incrementally push Japan, Taiwan, and even the United States out of regional influence",[20] thereby interestingly attaching a "hard" objective to China's "soft" power pursuit.

Both India and China are eager to play proactive roles in international affairs and are keen on building national images for communicating their confidence, willingness to open up and engage with the others, strength and readiness to contribute to global issues in a constructive fashion. However, it is important to highlight at this point that for soft power to work, national political and societal systems are greatly important in shaping overall narratives. While Beijing's "competitive state-led model and its authoritarian political system" obstruct a full capitalisation of its soft power, New Delhi suffers from adverse perceptions regarding the capacity of the Indian state to provide good governance and adequate public goods to its people.[21] On the other hand, in their strategies for employing soft power, India and China are heavily influenced by their respective histories: while China's notion of being the "Middle Kingdom" has greatly influenced its perception of the world, India's colonial past has determined its foreign policy trajectory and conditioned its interactions with the global community.[22]

Constructing a positive image has been an urgent strategic requirement for China given the negative image it has had for several years.[23] China's image-building efforts in modern times have no doubt imparted benign elements to its image, which have co-existed with an "assertive" strong persona. Perceptions about India have been different. Modern India's post-independence history has been important in this respect given India's choice to remain "non-aligned" and forge friendships for ensuring its pursuit of economic self-sufficiency without irking international or regional suspicion. Though cultural, or more specifically civilisational traits of the Indian state have not gone entirely unnoticed, India was never an aggressive user of cultural diplomacy (CD). However, as pointed out by David Malone, New Delhi's CD after independence and during the Cold War years towards Southeast Asia was perceived somewhat "gauche" by the countries, insofar as it seemed to suggest that some Southeast Asian countries were India's "cultural colonies".[24] This argument is examined later in this book in Chapters 2 and 3. Further, the Indian foreign policy initiatives, calling for Asian solidarity, actually met with little success in the region because the Southeast Asian nations had no desire to subordinate national identities to that of a greater Asian regional unity and disagreed with the claim that India was the "mother of all civilisations" in Asia. Moreover, India's poor economic performance earned New Delhi little respect from the "Asian tigers" (Hong Kong, Singapore, South Korea and Taiwan) that zoomed to prosperity on the basis of their neo-liberal outward-oriented economic policies that were very different from the inward-looking economic strategy being pursued by India post-independence.[25]

Perspective and policies have changed significantly over time. Greater economic globalisation and changes in outlooks to economic development have much to do with both India and China's urgencies to embark on proactive foreign policies emphasising effective communication and dialogue. Liberals like Polachek, Robst and Chang through their works[26] have rightly argued that growing inter-dependence in trade and finance would increasingly make wars obsolete. It is debatable if it has indeed been so. But there is no doubt about an economically interdependent world making cooperation critical for countries. As contemporary international relations have come to encounter new challenges (like terrorism), India and China have become more pragmatic with their priorities and mutual engagement, keeping in view their larger national objectives. Engaging with neighbours has become increasingly critical in this respect. While for China, Southeast Asia is its immediate periphery and therefore has been an important part of China's periphery diplomacy for several years – as will be discussed in Chapter 4 – India's emphatic engagement of the region is more recent. While the region is not India's immediate neighbourhood (except Myanmar which India share land and sea boundary), Southeast Asia has become crucial for India's economic development and strategic relevance. In this respect, the current Indian government's focus on the region reflects a continuation of the emphasis of its predecessors.[27]

Globalisation and interconnectedness have shrunk geographical spaces making image-building vital for communicating with others and thereby becoming strong determinants of geopolitics in the 21st century. Both India and China have been conscious of the salience of image-building in this regard, particularly for a region like Southeast Asia, which is an interesting comparative domain for studying relevant efforts of India and China.

China's pursuit of policies for building a positive global image is consistent with the enthusiasm of the Chinese imperial rulers, largely influenced by the philosophy of Confucius, in presenting China as a benevolent hegemon during the ancient times. In later years, the urge to communicate and build positive impressions was maintained through its first weekly periodical *Peking Review*, launched in March 1958, for enabling foreigners to know about China.[28] The Chinese Communist Party (CCP) has continued since with the task of building a positive global image by establishing the Overseas Propaganda Department under the Party Central Committee in 1990 followed by a new Information Office under the State Council in 1991 to communicate the nation's "true image" to the world.[29] In addition, prominent Chinese leaders like Li Peng and Jiang Zemin have consistently encouraged publicity for enhancing China's international image. Indeed, it is interesting to note that efforts have also been made to study external perceptions of China and the Chinese people for enabling official policies to differentiate, and apply more effective techniques for communicating with the global and domestic audiences with targets being different with different expectations.[30] *White Papers* and official reports are issued regularly by China for dissemination of the official Chinese position, often on sensitive issues like Tibet and Human Rights, and even on the One Belt One Road (OBOR),[31] aimed at the global audience, and ostensibly for image-building purposes. In a major effort aimed at consolidating image-building efforts, the Foreign Affairs Work Conference held in November 2014 dealt with all the aspects of China's foreign affairs in the civilian diplomatic sphere and was an attempt to outline and evaluate Beijing's foreign relations since the 18th Party Congress held in November 2012[32] partly to overcome China's image as being "non-transparent".

Building a positive national image, however, has not involved fundamental national sovereignty issues. Indeed, a positive image-building exercise has involved taking "strong" postures by governments on issues concerning sovereignty, while emphasising people-to-people collaboration and other similar partnerships for strengthening inter-state relationships. This has been evident with respect to both India and China. While both governments have been keen on image makeovers rooted in cooperation and partnership with neighbours, the leaderships haven't refrained from military options in national interest. The Indian army's surgical strike on terror launch pads across the Line of Control (LoC) in Pakistani territory in 2016 is a relevant example as it came after fairly extensive diplomatic engagement of Pakistan by India after the assumption of office by Prime Minister Modi. Similarly, in December 2016 China indicated its readiness to set up an Air Defence Identification Zone if Washington continued its military presence in the region.[33] Sending strong messages to the international audience is also a part of foreign policy pronouncements that are partly for domestic consumption as well. The citizens prefer their governments taking strong action when confronted by external challenges originating from outside the borders. This aspect, though, is beyond the scope of analysis of this book. The reference to the importance of "strong" communication is essentially to highlight the fact that image-building is a complex process and building national reputations are not exclusive of "hard" postures. Indeed, it involves both and is a fascinating aspect of foreign policymaking and diplomacy. Global leaders and national leaderships realise this synthesis and employ both aspects in their image-building efforts to communicate with the global audience.

SUMMARY OUTLINE: CHAPTERS

This book examines India and China's efforts at image-building in Southeast Asia for economic and strategic purposes. The region's economic dynamism combined with its geostrategic location has made it important for neighbours like India and China, as well as for extra-regional powers like the US. While Washington has been historically engaged with the region, Beijing's ancient ties with the Southeast Asian countries makes the strategic dynamics of the region complicated, which is compounded by large regional actors like India displaying active interest in engaging Southeast Asia. Both India and China have been employing a variety of soft power tools for deeper engagement with the region comprising eleven countries divided into the "mainland" (Myanmar, Thailand, Laos, Cambodia and Vietnam) and "island" zones (Malaysia, Singapore, Indonesia, the Philippines, Brunei and the new nation of East Timor, formerly part of Indonesia) with each country distinct in its economic activities and culture.[34] The region is strategically important for Australia, Japan and South Korea – three major actors of the Asia-Pacific – and countries with which India and China's relations have expanded over time. The book notes the significance of Australia, Japan and South Korea in the larger context of India and China's engagement of the region and reflects on the latter's engagement of the former contextually.

The next chapter, Chapter 2, outlines the main drivers behind India and China's engagement policies towards Southeast Asia while briefly examining historical ties between the region and India as well as between Southeast Asia and China. The historical links are important in the context of India's articulation of the Indo-Pacific framework, which has long-term significance for New Delhi's great power ambitions. On the other hand, China's engagement of Southeast Asia, as the book discusses, is partly driven by the "China dream" that has outlined Beijing's foreign policy since President Xi Jinping's assumption of power as the 7th President of the People's Republic of China in 2013. The historical presence of the US in Southeast Asia and the uncertainties regarding the nature of the US engagement in the region following the election of President Trump have also been discussed for enabling a clearer understanding of the regional dynamics.

Chapter 3 studies India's external outreach to Southeast Asia through the Look East Policy (LEP) that has been upgraded to the Act East Policy (AEP) by Prime Minister Narendra Modi's government. New Delhi's engagement with regional forums like the ASEAN has been discussed at length for highlighting the greater attention being devoted to the region. The China-US interface makes its strategic dynamics complex and challenging. It is important for New Delhi to remain involved in the region for communicating its intent of a bigger role in Southeast Asia commensurate with its size. India's multiple initiatives in the region, including connectivity and CD initiatives have also been analysed. All these initiatives are targeted at communicating with its extended neighbourhood for achieving its economic development while altering its image and establishing India's strategic influence.

Chapter 4 examines China's engagement with Southeast Asia through various soft power tools and also studies its attempts at regionalisation as well as recourse to multilateral diplomacy for foreign policy outreach. The chapter discusses at length the role of regional bodies like the Association of Southeast Asian Nations (ASEAN) in facilitating engagement through effective communication between Southeast Asian countries and China. The chapter attempts to analyse both China and the ASEAN's respective perceptions of each other while studying the engagement imperatives. China's latest strategic connectivity initiatives like the OBOR, also called the Belt and Road Initiative (BRI), is also examined along with other similar initiatives for integrating better with the region while facilitating international cooperation between China and its OBOR partners.

Both Chapters 3 and 4 also allude to the role of face-to-face diplomacy for enhanced cooperation and collaboration with neighbours by India and China. The key purpose of these visits has been to communicate messages for specific audiences. For example, international relations scholars view a simple handshake as an expression of many things including an informal contract, a simple greeting or sometimes even a battle for supremacy.[35] Scholars like Lebovic and Saunders argue that diplomatic interfaces might not create history, but facilitate conduct of foreign policy and diplomacy at the highest levels and are "primarily directed toward reinforcing relationships, communicating new information to old partners, and maintaining and promoting longstanding"[36] policies. Given the centrality of the high-level visits' in the conduct of diplomacy, the examples obtained from such diplomacy engaged in by senior Indian and Chinese leaders in Southeast Asia become an interesting framework for comparing image-building efforts. Finally, Chapter 5 is the concluding chapter and discusses India and China's approaches and challenges at building their respective national images in a region which is subject to an enormous variety of complex internal challenges and external predicaments.

ENDNOTES

1. *The Great Illusion*
2. 'China celebrates 70 years since victory over Japan'
3. Palit, Sinha, 'China-India communication'
4. 'What were the causes of the Peloponnesian war?'
5. Oldemeinen, 'The Political Realism of Thucydides and Thomas'
6. 'India is a messenger of world peace', *Mann ki Baat*, 29 October 2017 at http://www.thehindu.com/news/national/mann-ki-baatindia-is-a-messenger-of-world-peace-says-modi/article19943906.ece (Accessed 31 October 2017)
7. Ruggiero, 'Mill's Principle of Intellectual Humility'
8. Keaney, 'The Realism of Hans Morgenthau'
9. Nation branding
10. White, 'Brands and national image: an exploration of inverse country-of-origin effect'
11. For years, International Relations comprised largely of two more dominant approaches: the theory of realism, and liberalism/pluralism. Over time a new theory – constructivism – began to develop focusing on ideas of norms, the development of structures, the relationship between actors and said structures, as well as how identity influences actions and behaviour amongst and between actors, with norms themselves shaping an actor's character. For details see 'Constructivism in International Relations'
12. Nye, *The Future of Power*: 51
13. Arndt, *The First Resort of Kings*: 3
14. For details see Palit, Sinha, *Analysing China's Soft Power Strategy*
15. Farewell, *Persuasion and Power*: XIX
16. Faulkner, 'The official truth: Propaganda in the Ancient Roman Empire'
17. Farewell: 57
18. Ibid
19. Kurlantzick, 'China's Charm: Implications of Chinese Soft Power'
20. Ibid
21. Palit, Sinha, *Analysing China's Soft Power Strategy*
22. Ibid
23. China's "isolation" under Mao Tse Tung greatly led to international suspicion about Beijing. Subsequently, its policies and particularly the Tiananmen Square incident in 1989 fuelled an active discourse on China during the mid-1990s, characterising it as a "destabilising force" along with proliferation of "China collapse" theories. Such cynical portrayals of China drove it to work on its global image with Chinese experts focusing on those aspects of China they felt were virtuous and attractive to the international community. The efforts became part

of the Chinese idea of comprehensive national power born in the late 1990s, emphasising technological and economic capacities along with national cohesion. See Deng, 'The New Hard Realities': 66

24. Malone, 'Soft power in Indian foreign policy'
25. Ibid
26. Polachek, 'Liberalism and Interdependence: Extending the Trade-Conict Model': 405-422
27. India's Look East policy (LEP) was initiated by PV Narasimha Rao in 1991 and then followed by successive governments led by AB Vajpayee and Manmohan Singh.
28. Hongying, 'National image building and Chinese foreign policy'
29. Ibid
30. Ibid
31. The first action plan on the OBOR was articulated through the 'Vision and Actions on Jointly Building Silk Road Economic Belt and 21st-Century Maritime Silk Road' in March 2015 communicating the ancient Silk Road spirit – 'peace and cooperation, openness and inclusiveness, mutual learning and mutual benefit'. For details see 'Vision and Actions on Jointly Building Silk Road Economic Belt and 21st-Century Maritime Silk Road'
32. 'The Central Conference on Work relating to Foreign Affairs was held in Beijing'
33. Panos, 'South China Sea: Beijing sends a strong message to America and Taiwan'
34. However, East Timor is not a part of the Association of Southeast Asian Nations (ASEAN) and the analysis in the book does not extend to China and India's ties with East Timor
35. Fu, Jing, 'Handshakes symbolise Xi's new era': 21
36. Lebovic, 'The Diplomatic Core: How the United States employs High-level visits as a scarce resource'

2

Southeast Asia's Strategic Significance: Extra-Regional Perspective

With Asia poised to be the new theatre of power given its sustained, rapid economic growth for several decades and its undisputed role as an engine for the world economy, Asian powers like India and China are now global actors with consummate strategic outreach. The end of the Cold War signalled the readiness of the international community to accommodate "emerging" powers for redefining international relations. India, China (and Brazil) can indeed be considered "great powers" if geographical size and large economies are determinants of "great powers".[1] The American political scientist Lustick argues that while China is already recognised a major power (and Brazil choosing to remain in the US orbit rather than asserting itself as an independent power), it is only "India which can be genuinely regarded as pursuing the search with some degree of determination and is therefore deserving of study by its very exceptionalism in the contemporary era".[2]

Both India and China are influencing world affairs and communicating their inclination to keep doing so in line with the shift in the global economic centre of gravity from the West to the East. While many argue that it is premature or an exaggeration to conclude that Asia will emerge as the world's predominant power player,[3] there is little doubt about the emergence of the region as a force to reckon with.[4]

With China emerging as a politico-military actor, Asia has become particularly significant in the American strategic calculus with the US having reaffirmed its focus on the region given its geostrategic interest in Asia reflected in President Obama's "pivot to Asia" strategy. The Donald Trump Presidency, however, might see major changes in the nature and intensity of US involvement with the region.

Southeast Asia[5] in Asia is a vital region for both India and China (and therefore additionally for extra-regional actors like the US that are aware of the strategic ripples generated in the region by major power ambitions of both). The region encompasses vibrant middle-income economies (Malaysia, Thailand, Indonesia and Philippines) along with industrially mature (or resource rich) high-income economies (e.g. Brunei, Singapore) and lower income economies with bright prospects (Vietnam, Cambodia, Myanmar and Lao PDR). The regional economies are deeply integrated with each other as well as with global trade and investment flows. The countries comprise the regional cooperation framework of Association of Southeast Asian Nations, or the ASEAN, which came into being in 1967.[6] The region is strategically significant as a maritime geography spanning across South China Sea, the Indian Ocean and the Bay of Bengal that has emerged as one of the busiest shipping routes of the world connecting the Americas with Asia. With shipping routes like the Strait of Malacca ferrying huge energy and goods cargo back and forth, the geostrategic value of the region becomes significant for neighbourhood actors like China, Japan, South Korea, Australia and India, as well as extra-regional powers – the US and Europe. Economic resources like oil and gas that remain unexploited in the maritime depths of the region further enhance its significance.

It is hardly surprising therefore that regional and extra-regional powers are vying for larger roles in Southeast Asia leading to occasional near-conflict situations. The existence of multiple contesting powers in Southeast Asia and historical territorial disputes in the South China Sea are responsible for heightened power politics in the region. While China has been a historical player in Southeast Asia, the US military presence in the region[7] which is deemed to be China's "zone of influence", adds complexity to the regional power dynamics. The complications are compounded by India's desire to play an active role in regional politics. While India's growing influence exacerbates the Sino-Indian strategic competition in the region, the rivalry is hardly as intense as the US-China contest. As if Beijing-Washington and New Delhi's turf battles for strategic space in Southeast Asia were not enough, Canberra's strategic "reevaluation" of the region in recent years[8] enhances the number of actors and strategic perspectives in the regional matrix. Relations between these actors are major sources of consternation for the region, such as the Sino-Japan hostilities, which might have encouraged Tokyo to use Southeast Asia as a "diplomatic and economic hedge against China"[9] by taking more pronounced interest in regional affairs. This chapter, in the context of this remarkably complicated strategic environment of the region, reflects briefly on its ancient links with India and China for better understanding of the contemporary strategic activism of both countries in the region. It also analyses the role of Washington as an extra-regional actor in shaping China's focus on the region.

INDIA-SOUTHEAST ASIA ENGAGEMENT: HISTORY AND *REALPOLITIK*

While KM Panikkar, the eminent scholar of India's maritime strategy, had conveyed Southeast Asia's strategic relevance to India through his work,[10] the region hardly figured prominently in India's foreign policy. It is only since the 1990s that Indian commentators began indicating that "India should break out of the claustrophobic confines of South Asia"[11] for achieving larger strategic objectives that necessitated restoration of ties with Southeast Asia. As a result, from being of marginal importance, the region gradually rose in prominence in India's foreign policy. India's geographical proximity to the region, particularly shared land and maritime boundaries with some Southeast Asian countries,[12] along with the relevance of the region in broader issues of development and security, has led to its figuring in India's extended neighbourhood policy. India's increasing economic, naval and military capacities along with its great power ambition have been driving its engagement of Southeast Asia reflecting a "natural" expansion of its strategic space.[13]

With the term "Indo-Pacific"[14] gaining strategic traction in India, New Delhi's economic growth and its future prospects have got firmly linked to the Indo-Pacific region making India a stakeholder in the region's security and stability. Needless to say, the Indo-Pacific fits well in New Delhi's vision of an "extended neighbourhood" given that it helps in introducing a counterbalancing dimension to the growing Chinese presence in the Indian Ocean. Consequently, India is seeking to deepen its engagement with countries in Southeast Asia and further beyond in the Asia-Pacific like Australia and Japan, thus making such engagements critical. In fact, Canberra's growing interface with New Delhi is already seen maturing in this regard. Australia's *Defence White Paper* 2016 has considered India a partner with which Canberra shares "key interests in regional stability and order" across the Indo-Pacific, apart from calling India a strong player whose activism in the Indian Ocean has been encouraged: "In addition to having a stronger role in the Indo-Pacific region, India is also likely to become a more active and influential global power, supported by its economic growth" with which Australia wants to "strengthen our cooperation in maritime security...".[15] The maritime security angle is increasingly getting countries in Asia together with India assuming a big power role in the region.

India's deep historical links with Southeast Asia also provide a natural context for its contemporary engagement. India's relations with Southeast Asia have centred on economic, religious and cultural interfaces, dating back to the Mauryan period (r. ca. 273-232 BC) when trade facilitated the export of Indian culture, religion, spiritual practices, social customs, language, art, architecture, epic narrative and more.[16] Though scholars like Malone point out that Southeast Asian countries thought that there was a possibility of India perceiving them as its "cultural colonies" after India achieved its independence,[17] historically ancient India's cultural influence was quite different. The cultural exchanges were "peaceful" and bereft of imperialist intentions. Scholars like Van Leur have established how the "Indianisation" of Southeast Asia was devoid of conquests and colonisation and was limited to cultural intercourse only. The postulate is based on the evidence that Southeast Asian rulers "borrowed" Indian ideas and modified them to adapt and apply them locally for enhancing their own authority and legitimacy and also enable the establishment of a political organisation.[18] Many scholars have highlighted this "Indian" adaptation in Southeast Asia in complete contrast to similar examples from China. According to George Coedes, an eminent scholar on classical Southeast Asia, while the Chinese emperors demanded the "Southern barbarians" to acknowledge their authority by sending them regular tributes, the Indian rulers focused on exchanges of embassies between the two shores of the Bay of Bengal based on equality.[19]

India's "peaceful" cultural and religious penetration in the region has been further emphasised by several scholars who draw attention to the facilitating role Indian Muslim traders and missionaries played in spreading Islamist cultures and beliefs in the region.[20] Indian influence in various aspects of Southeast Asian lives is indeed "loaned" as against "imposed". David Malone describes it quite succinctly:[21]

> 'great Indinanised kingdoms arose over the centuries throughout Asia and particularly Southeast Asia.... [following] Indian court customs, administrative organisation on the Indian pattern, and laws based on the Code of Manu, the Indian lawgiver. Indianisation also included the alphabetical basis of Southeast Asian scripts, the incorporation of Sanskrit in vocabularies along with adoption of the Hindu-Buddhist religious beliefs, and an Indian concept of royalty.'

There are, however, scholars pointing to the non-"peaceful" interaction of India with the region as well like the invasion of the Srivijaya kingdom in Sumatra in the 11th century CE by the Chola monarch Rajendra. While the invasion might have been precipitated by economic factors, many argue that the expansionist intentions cannot be entirely discarded.[22]

India and Southeast Asia Post-1947

Even before India's independence in August 1947, the interim government led by Jawaharlal Nehru organised the "Conference on Asian Relations" in March 1947 underlining India's keenness on engaging the region. Nehru's *The Discovery of India* published in 1946 referred to Southeast Asia as "Greater India" highlighting his (and the Indian leadership's) idea of the region as a part of India flowing from ancient links and the profound but predominantly "ideational" Indian influence. The engagement, however, became stunted in the decades that followed, largely due to India's pursuit of inward-looking economic policies which was in marked contrast to the policies being followed by most of Southeast Asia. The resultant regional perception of India discouraged greater interface and was characterised by reluctance in forging closer ties. The reluctance persisted throughout the Cold War decades as India's commitment to non-alignment and subsequent proximity with the erstwhile Soviet Union kept it at arm's length from the region. It was not until the early 1990s and the implementation of outward-oriented economic policies followed by the pronouncement of the LEP by the then Prime Minister PV Narasimha Rao that Southeast Asia began obtaining greater attention from India and began reciprocating the same.

The Indian leadership's ideological focus prevented greater engagement with Southeast Asia during the Cold War years, notwithstanding Nehru's vision of the region being "Greater India". The ideological underpinning of India's engagement strategy with the region has been steadily replaced by greater pragmatism since the 1990s. While economics has largely fashioned India's approach to engagement, its intent to play a bigger role in regional and global affairs has also been important in fostering closer interaction with Southeast Asia. Apart from being a significant geostrategic entity demanding greater interface, Southeast Asia also provides India the opportunity of connecting economically with other important powers in the region, such as Australia[23] and Japan. India's strong economic performance since the 1990s has made it conscious about the importance of maintaining peace and stability in the neighbourhood, including in the maritime space. Southeast Asia's pivotal maritime location not only makes it a vital region for India in pursuing its economic progress but a stakeholder as well in safeguarding the region's security. Indeed, a host of factors including geography, economics, security, cultivation of new regional alliances involving partners like Australia, Japan and South Korea, and last, but not the least, the emerging strategic construct of the "Indo-Pacific" has compelled India to interact more closely with the region. These are discussed in greater detail below.

Securing the Sea Lanes of Communication (SLOC): Enhancing security of the SLOC through Southeast Asia has been a major imperative for India. India's increasing dependence on maritime traffic through Southeast Asia, particularly the Malacca Strait, for energy supplies and other commodity trade, has made it sensitive to the security of the global commons[24] and the same a major policy priority.[25] India's naval diplomacy in the Malacca Strait has its roots in the LEP. India has not only helped patrol the Strait on behalf of Indonesia and Malaysia[26] but has also been partnering the US in its joint patrols, thus endorsing its "claim that its security interests stretch up to and include the straits".[27] Connected to the overall security of the seas are the other major problems like human trafficking and smuggling of small arms and drugs through the seas that not only concern India but the other countries of the region as well.

Enabling Geographic Location: Several countries of the region have geographical significance for India in multiple respects. Myanmar, for example, is a country that shares both land and sea borders with India providing gateways to the region and beyond by connecting India's northeast to Southeast Asia. Similarly Thailand, its strategic location on the rim of the Bay of Bengal and the access it provides to the Indian Ocean and the South China Sea, is also an important country given its shared maritime boundary with India, connecting it to the other Southeast Asian neighbours like Cambodia and Vietnam. Apart from the economic and connectivity opportunities that both Myanmar and Thailand offer, their geographical contiguity makes them important countries from an Indian security perspective. Transit of arms and drugs across the Myanmar border and the erstwhile military junta's ambivalent approach towards the militants operating in the region[28] have been a source of concern for India, leading to occasional precipitate action. The surgical strike inside Myanmar in June 2015 to flush out insurgents was one such Indian military action which was widely criticised as "the Indian government's 'chest-thumping' over the successful covert operation".[29]

Malaysia – another country being engaged partly for its geographic location – is situated at the tip of the Straits of Malacca and offers the shortest sea route between the Persian Gulf and other major Asian economies – notably China, Japan, South Korea and the Pacific Rim, apart from India.[30] Malaysia also acts as the crucial maritime linkage between the Indian Ocean, the South China Sea and the Pacific Ocean.[31] Singapore is another country with great geo-economic significance for India, given its role in re-exporting and transit of goods and people between India and the rest of the Asia-Pacific. Indonesia, on the other hand, the world's largest archipelagic state and the biggest country of the region, owns three of the four Southeast Asian straits through which 38 per cent of the world's sea-borne trade passes.[32] Indonesia is one of the most significant geostrategic actors in the Indian Ocean and is critical for India in terms of the latter's efforts to retain strategic influence in the region and also connecting it to another major Indian Ocean actor – Australia. The Indonesian leadership's plan to posit itself as the global maritime axis[33] by promoting connectivity between the Indian Ocean and the Pacific make it a vital partner in India's long-term strategic and maritime vision for the Asia-Pacific.

Natural Resources: Southeast Asia has large reserves of energy and natural resources that have increased its strategic appeal to neighbours like India and China. Close ties with Myanmar – a major source of energy resources – become important for India given that access to Myanmar's energy resources greatly enhances India's prospects in regional energy trade as Myanmar is on the transit route between India and the rest of Southeast Asia.[34] Indonesia's natural resources are varied and abundant with palm oil, rubber, cocoa, coffee, nickel and copper, marine reserves of hydrothermal sulphides containing gold, silver, copper, lead and zinc, and, of course, crude oil. Malaysia is almost similarly endowed in resources, making both countries coveted for India and other major powers. Energy resources are also pulling India close to Vietnam, one of the largest sources of oil in the region.[35] Laos, one of the relatively smaller and economically backward countries in the region, has considerable potential for generation of hydel power emanating from the Mekong River and its tributaries, which has prompted India to deepen engagement with the country. Rich in oil and gas reserves, India is also visualising a greater cooperation with Brunei. Finally Singapore, while not being a custodian of crude or untapped energy and natural resources, is nonetheless one of the largest hubs of oil refining in the region and a vital cog in India's energy trade with the Asia-Pacific.

Market and Capacity: Southeast Asian markets are important economic prospects for India. From a wider regional perspective, the establishment of the ASEAN Economic Community (AEC) in 2015 and its move towards a single market and production base besides "a competitive economic region of equitable economic development and a region fully integrated into the global economy",[36] signals new opportunities for India. Individually, apart from Singapore and Malaysia, which are among India's major trade partners, a country like Vietnam has increasingly emerged as a significant market for India. Vietnam's rapid economic progress and proficiency in the production of garments makes it capable of absorbing large imports of fabric and yarn from India while exporting its lower priced garments to the expanding Indian market and augmenting bilateral intra-industry trade.[37] Over the years, Vietnam has also emerged as a major market for India's indigenous defence exports.[38] Thailand, while being another of India's major trade partners from the region, has helped India in integrating with the regional automobile supply chains by being a major supplier of auto parts to India, and increasingly becoming an important market for the cars assembled in India.

Various Indian exports to Cambodia like pharmaceuticals, textiles and leather goods are also increasing. Like Vietnam, Cambodia is another country in the region that can emerge as a major market for Indian manufactured exports. Indeed, India's efforts to locate convenient manufacturing "hubs" in the region for its investors make Cambodia along with Myanmar, Laos and Vietnam a highly attractive proposition. Prospects of markets with good economic opportunities extend to Philippines as well, where the former President Aquino's "Universal Health" policy had opened the way for an invigorated partnership with the pharmaceutical sector in India, particularly with regard to generics, for providing quality medicines at affordable prices.[39]

The economic opportunities for India with respect to Southeast Asia are not limited to only new markets and export prospects but also to capacity building. Singapore is a pertinent example. Ranked consistently among the world's topmost countries for doing business, Singapore has become the largest source of inward FDI into India overtaking Mauritius.[40] It is regarded as a country that can not only get investments into India but also high-class human resource systems and practices that can be of great help in skilling India's huge young population. Its reputed skill development institutions like the Institute of Technical Education (ITE) can be useful in this regard. Indeed wishfully, an ITE-type institution in each Indian state would transform India's skills landscape.[41] In addition to skills, Singapore's facilities are also coming in considerable use for Indian businesses and professionals with its fast and efficient legal infrastructure enabling Indian companies to participate in several arbitrations and its sophisticated financial agencies and institutions allowing Indian companies to efficiently do business with other parts of Southeast Asia and Asia-Pacific by using Singapore as a gateway.

Strategic Rivalry with China: India's growing preoccupation with Southeast Asia has also been influenced by the heightened assertiveness of China in the region, resultant tensions, and the possibility of increasing strategic influence by being a counterbalance to China. In more recent years, the Indian tendency for contesting Chinese influence has been strengthened by the expansion of China's military presence, diplomacy and strategic reach in the Indian Ocean, which has aggravated India's security concerns in its backyard. Given the prominence of the Indo-Pacific architecture in India's strategic vision, Southeast Asia – a part of the world where China is the largest extra-regional actor with outstanding territorial disputes and hostilities with various countries – India's efforts to measure up to Chinese influence is natural. This might result in India becoming more active in supporting countries like Vietnam that are embroiled in disputes with China in the South China Sea. Malaysia – another country that has maritime dispute with China – has recently embarked on a maritime security partnership with India.[42] In fact, the defence cooperation between India and Malaysia is mainly in the maritime arena. The Joint Statement signed during Malaysian Prime Minister Najib's visit to India in 2017 underlined the proposal for Navy-to-Navy field exercises between the two countries. India and Singapore in a Joint Statement in 2015 had also decided to expand their cooperation in maritime security.[43] Maritime cooperation is also high on the agenda between India and Indonesia with both the countries recognising the preeminence of the maritime domain in the relationship. Both the leaders had released a separate statement in 2016, dealing only with maritime cooperation in addition to a Joint Statement.[44]

While Malaysia has been a "natural stepping stone" to ASEAN for India, Vietnam too has been its strategic advocate within the ASEAN and has been the country coordinator for India from 2015 to 2018.[45] With China launching the OBOR – a diplomatic and economic programme that could significantly alter the regional economic and strategic orders – India and some Southeast Asian countries, worried over the rapid expansion of Chinese influence in the region, might inch closer in the long-run.[46]

Deeper Engagement with Asia-Pacific: The Southeast Asian region provides India the access to the rest of the Asia-Pacific region, particularly with countries like Australia, Japan and South Korea for deepening economic and security relations. A deeper engagement with the Asia-Pacific is an important objective in New Delhi's "Act East" policy initiated by Prime Minister Narendra Modi. Australia and Japan have been the driving forces behind the establishment of the Asia Pacific Economic Cooperation (APEC) in 1989 for facilitating trade and economic integration within the region. India was not included in the APEC since its economy was still inward-looking at that time and was thus inconsistent with the Grouping's objective of free and open trade and investment. But post-India's liberalisation policy, India has been keen on becoming a member of the APEC, an interest that has been welcomed by the US[47] and other major APEC members. India's recent activism in the region is in line with this interest, prompted by greater economic linkages with the Asia Pacific as well as security and strategic interests. In this respect, it is hardly surprising to note the prominence of "Indo-Pacific" in India's contemporary strategic discourse. India is clearly keen on playing a major role in the "Indo-Pacific" by establishing a larger framework of cooperation with Australia and Indonesia. The troika of India, Indonesia and Australia announced in 2012 is a case in point.[48] Apart from a closer security cooperation with Australia and Indonesia, India's security partnerships with Japan and

South Korea also reflect the significance it attaches to partnerships in the Asia-Pacific.

Diaspora: As part of its larger public diplomacy efforts, India has begun engaging its diaspora in various parts of the world, including in Southeast Asia. The Indian-origin population is sizeable in Malaysia[49] and Singapore and is also increasing elsewhere in the region due to a greater movement of skilled Indians in the last couple of decades. Cultivating the Indian diaspora in the region is important both for economic gains such as tourism and investments, and also for strategic benefits that can arise from the facilitating role played by the diaspora in bringing India and their resident countries closer. Modi's visits to countries like Singapore can be seen as efforts to engage the diaspora in a region whose economic power can not only help shape India's economic growth and propel its Make in India initiative,[50] but assist India's image-building efforts as well. Interestingly, when Modi addressed the Indian diaspora in Singapore in November 2015, he praised it for contributing effectively to India's positive image: "The entire world is reposing a lot of faith in India today and the reason behind this is not Modi, but the Indians settled abroad".[51] These efforts at a greater engagement of the diaspora have received a major impetus in the last few years and especially under Prime Minister Modi.

China-Southeast Asia Engagement: Periphery Diplomacy and "China Dream"

The 16th Party Congress in 2002 first highlighted China's focus on its periphery when it was described as being of "primary importance" in China's foreign policy matrix.[52] Subsequently, the term has evolved and gained traction in Beijing's external engagement policy with the former Premier Wen Jiabao coining the concepts of "good neighbourhood, secure neighbourhood, and wealthy neighbourhood" a year later in 2003.[53] Since then, the periphery and Southeast Asia has gained immense attention among Chinese academics with many scholars even viewing Southeast Asia as a "shifting zone of interaction" for two reasons: the "contestation over sovereignty claims in the South China Sea between China and the littoral states" and "because of pressures to expand the boundaries beyond the region to a wider East Asian setting".[54] China's engagement of the region is therefore multi-pronged and have other dimensions to it as well. A peaceful external environment will not only help the leadership to focus on the economic development of its people but could be a testing ground for its great power ambitions. Similarly, the rich resources of the region and increased trade and market opportunities with the countries in Southeast Asia will facilitate its rejuvenation and reemergence at the global stage.

Beijing's historical interpretation of Southeast Asia as its traditional sphere of influence has a bearing on its ambition to play the role of a great regional power, prompting its revisionist tendencies in the region. Its historical links with the region are in contrast to those of India. China's focus on Southeast Asia is not new and dates back several centuries in history. The exploits of Admiral Zheng He, who commanded seven voyages of trade and discovery in Southeast and South Asian waters (1405-1433) during the Ming dynasty, is repeatedly referred to by the Chinese leadership as a symbol of China's "benign" naval dominance of the region. Apart from "peaceful" naval expeditions undertaken during the ancient times, China's interactions with countries like Vietnam and Myanmar were through the framework of the "tributary system" during the pre-colonial times. According to Min Shu, "Southeast Asia had long been an integral part of the China-centred tribute system".[55] However, Imperial China's concept of the tributary state system[56] is unlike other tributary systems as comprehended by scholastic interpretations in the West. The system is unique and akin to father-son relationship with the association "unequal" but "benign" like in an ideal Confucian family.[57] The tribute system or more generally the *tianxia* (all under the heaven),[58] which is an important feature of the tributary system, integrated morality with power shaping China's foreign policy and trade with the neighbourhood for two centuries. Chinese scholars and academics have emphasised the concept for highlighting ancient China's emphasis on cooperation and harmony, devoid of hegemony.

A contemporary Chinese scholar, Zhao Tingyang, theorises *tianxia* by illustrating "soft" dimensions of Chinese strategic thinking that rejects hegemony, exclusion of people, individual interests and "internationality"[59] and offers an alternate image of contemporary China. Both the tribute system and *tianxia* are projected as being integral to China's "peaceful rise". However, there are contrasting views regarding *tianxia* as well, particularly from scholars like William Callahan who argue that "rather than guide us toward a post-hegemonic world order, *tianxia* presents a new hegemony where imperial China's hierarchical governance is updated for the twenty-first century".[60]

Notwithstanding Southeast Asia's ancient ties with China, the colonial era, the rise of Japan and the outbreak of the Second World War weakened its influence on the region. In fact, China's focus on the region was shaped by its involvement in various regional developments in the periphery such as the First Indochina War (1946-54),[61] the Korean War (1950-53),[62] and the emergence of rival Communist forces in Cambodia. The period from the 1950s to the early 1970s also witnessed Beijing's pursuit of a revolutionary foreign policy posture in the neighbourhood with China extending military, political and propaganda support to rebel groups in Southeast Asian countries like Cambodia and Indonesia, which heavily tarnished China's global reputation as attempts to export Communism in the neighbourhood and unsettle the non-Communist states of the region.

In more recent times, the presence of an extra-regional power (the US) trying to "rebalance" the power play in Southeast Asia by matching resources with China in its "traditional sphere of influence" (Southeast Asia) has created discomfort for the Chinese leadership. This is discussed in greater detail later. Indeed, a greater influence of the regional powers like Australia and Japan on the region and the concomitant complications in regional dynamics has further conditioned China's diplomatic behaviour towards Southeast Asia.

China's rapid economic progress has enabled it to leverage a closer economic collaboration for securing strategic gains from the region. Beijing has used economic collaboration not only to "pressure ASEAN governments into tightening their 'One China' policies" but also sought their support for its strategies towards Tibet and Xinjiang.[63] China's realisation of a US and West-dominated international order emphasising global integration being in sharp contrast to a China-centric world order has encouraged Beijing to pursue a "positive" strategy for deeper economic linkage and garnering of goodwill amongst its immediate neighbours for facilitating its "rise". Given the importance of a peaceful benign external environment for facilitating its ascent, Beijing hasn't spared efforts to assure neighbours about economic cooperation, thereby forestalling resistance to its rise in the long run.[64] The assurance is visible again in the OBOR initiative: "China has tried to adjust its approaches to convince Southeast Asian countries that the OBOR initiative holds potential synergy with ASEAN's development strategies and can play a complementary role in the building of the ASEAN Community".[65] The Chinese strategy in this respect is reflective of the importance it attaches to relationship-building with neighbours in its efforts to achieve great power status. But while emphasising cooperation, Beijing is also particular in extending power exercises in the region in a fashion that it believes will be critical in determining its relations with the US.[66] Such aspirations are in addition to China's economic interests in engaging Southeast Asia, particularly its need to access energy resources, which necessitates the maintenance of a stable political climate in the region. The rich energy resources in the South China Sea, the rich fishing grounds and the strategic importance of the region as SLOC further prompt Beijing's focus on the region. Indeed, engaging Southeast Asia is consistent with the priorities outlined in President Xi's signature narrative of the "China Dream" that underscores safeguarding sovereignty, ensuring domestic stability and economic progress as key objectives of engaging neighbours in a bid to maintain its prominence in the world order.

China Dream **(zhong guo meng)** *and Southeast Asia*

The "China Dream", symbolising policy priorities of the fifth generation Communist Party of China (CPC) leadership under President Xi, was first articulated during the President's keynote speech at the National People's Congress (NPC) in March 2013: "the Chinese dream, after all, is the dream of the people... We must incessantly *bring benefits to the people* (emphasis added)".[67] Acquiring wide attention from the local and global media, the "China Dream" has become a much-discussed phrase ever since. Apart from rejuvenating China, the "China Dream" is an end by itself. The welfare of the Chinese people is central to the vision of a strong China, as aspired in the Dream. While its specifics were not spelt out by President Xi in his address, the vision is becoming clearer over time as policy directions reveal more about its goals. The three key priorities appear to be *economic growth* facilitated and maximised by a benign neighbourhood, *safeguarding national sovereignty* and *minimising threats to internal stability*. The priorities had resonated in the Third Plenary Session of the 18th CPC Central Committee in November 2013 that focused on comprehensive reforms and opening up.[68]

A peaceful external environment is essential for *sustained economic progress* manifesting in better living standards of the people. China's "peaceful development" strategy, amended from "peaceful rise",[69] is a conscious correction for avoiding intimidating perceptions associated with "rise", and is expected to contribute significantly to the establishment of a benign environment. The strategy, introduced by the fourth generation Hu-Wen leadership, is being persisted with by the current generation. At a press briefing in March 2013, Premier Li Keqiang commented "even if China becomes stronger, we will not seek hegemony".[70] What he did not mention was that Beijing's commitment to "peaceful development" would not, under any circumstances, imply compromising on national sovereignty issues. *Safeguarding sovereignty* is a major focus of the leadership and a vital component in the China Dream. The focus warrants close attention and engagement of the periphery such as Southeast Asia as China aspires to become a maritime power with access to, and control over, neighbourhood sea lanes. Outstanding maritime disputes between China and Southeast Asian countries influence the extent by which China obtains such access and control in the South China Sea with implications for safeguarding sovereignty.

The present Chinese leadership has made it abundantly clear that China is sensitive to issues of sovereignty and would not consider compromises. Interacting with members of the ruling CPC's inner elite in July 2013, President Xi made it clear that "in no way will the country abandon its legitimate rights and interests, nor will it give up its core national interests".[71] China's sovereignty issue has been most apparent with its neighbours over the South China Sea dispute. In the wake of the ruling in the arbitration case that the Philippines had unilaterally initiated against China in 2016, President Xi announced that "no foreign country should expect us to swallow the bitter fruit of damage to our sovereignty, security and development interests".[72] The sentiment is also reflected in the Chinese Navy's efforts to expand its outreach. The remarks of a former Navy political commissar and the current deputy head of the Foreign Affairs Committee of the NPC on the sidelines of the NPC Meet in March 2017 that China would build a larger navy roster since the Navy will play a bigger role in defending the country's maritime rights and interests,[73] underscores Beijing's current focus on further strengthening its maritime capability. In this regard, China's proclivity would be to settle issues bilaterally with other countries and the leadership would not hesitate to take strong positions, if necessary. The Chinese leadership's complete dismissal of the Hague arbitration in 2016 on the country's long-running dispute with the Philippines while "committing to peace",[74] is a case in point.

A strategy of bilateral consultation combined with an assertive posture appears to be the main plank of China's approach towards settling sovereignty issues in its periphery. Its intention to be assertive is evident from the rapid upgrading of its military hardware. As a region experiencing a manifestation of the sovereignty focus in the China Dream, Southeast Asia would see greater applications of consultative and assertive postures marking the co-existence of "soft" and "hard" elements in Chinese engagement policies. Indeed, China's call for deeper engagement with neighbours and advocating multi-country frameworks for regional solutions like the Code of Conduct (COC) for the South China Sea, are unlikely to be accompanied by intentions to yield ground on existing territorial disputes.

Alongside territorial sovereignty, *preserving internal security and stability* are equally significant imperatives for China. Ethnic clashes in the Xinjiang Uighur Autonomous Region, China's largest administrative division, have been major concerns for the Chinese leadership as they can undermine "stability above all else" for achieving the China Dream. A peaceful development strategy for engaging neighbours should have positive spinoffs for domestic stability too. Engaging Southeast Asia that has a sizeable Muslim population in many countries (e.g. Malaysia, Indonesia and Brunei) can be effective in communicating positive signals to unhappy domestic constituencies like the Uighurs.

Finally, Southeast Asia becomes critical in balancing the US interest in the region, which became particularly pronounced during the former US President Obama's "pivot to Asia" strategy. The absence of President Obama at the 21st Economic Leaders' Meeting of the APEC in Bali in October 2013 had offered China an important opportunity for expanding its engagement with the region and invigorating its strategic presence given the void created by his absence. President Xi was quick to seize the opportunity by upping the ante. While economic co-development was firmly stressed, he also reiterated China's commitment to peace and stability in the region: "China will firmly uphold regional peace and stability... without peace, development is out of the question, like water without a source or a tree without roots". Notwithstanding the change in US administration and President Donald Trump at the helm of affairs, China's efforts to push for a deeper economic cooperation for maintaining strategic influence aiming to neutralise the US, should persist in the foreseeable future.

US and Southeast Asia: Complicating Dynamics

The US foreign policy community, for whom Southeast Asia has been salient for long given its involvement with the region during the Cold War years, has argued that the US leadership has not demonstrated enough enthusiasm to engage the region. While calling for stepping up engagement with the ASEAN countries, it has held that:[75]

> The American experience in Asia suggests that inattention to dynamics and trends in the region and insensitivity to the contours of national and regional pride and desires are an unnecessary recipe for resentment and conflict. It is in the national interest to prudently commit a larger share of our national attention and our national resources to Southeast Asia.

Washington's attention with Southeast Asia does reflect inconsistencies. The Treaty of Mutual Cooperation and Security signed by the US and

Japan in 1952 is the cornerstone of Washington's security policy in Asia. Its involvement in the Vietnam war during the 1950s and 1960s, its failure to prevent Communists from assuming political authority in Vietnam, and the genocide in Cambodia later, have been instrumental in shaping the US foreign policy trajectory towards Southeast Asia during the time. Though the incidents made the US leadership wary of a proactive involvement in Southeast Asia, the US policymakers nonetheless tried to maintain the influence Washington had gained in the region during Word War II. Washington forged defense alliances with many Southeast Asian countries like the Philippines during the early Cold War days while promoting free trade with many after the end of the Cold War. However, at the same time, much of the engagement was left to its key ally Japan, particularly for strengthening the ASEAN's institutions. Indeed, Southeast Asia has been a prominent component of the US-Japan security alliance. It has been argued that:[76]

> For both allies, more sophisticated understanding of and multilayered engagement with Southeast Asia is necessary. They share a stake and a responsibility to encourage one another in this effort. At its core, this effort must be supported by a clearer domestic political consensus than now exists in either country that investing in ASEAN economically and from a security perspective is a core national security mandate.

Notwithstanding the strategic benefits that Washington obtained from Japan's overarching economic presence in the region, the US approach was forced to change after the Asian financial crisis of 1997 and the global economic crisis of 2008. Both crises significantly reduced Japan's economic clout and strategic control of the region. More importantly, both calamities found China's economic rise unaffected. China's growing geostrategic influence over the region produced by its economic rise and integration with Southeast Asia made the US conscious not only of China's assertive tendencies, but also its efforts to establish a Sino-centric model for Asian economic development[77] and security.[78] Uncertain of the then "pivot", and a "risk-acceptant power"[79] with both economic and military clout ensuring its inordinate influence, the US began revisiting its strategy towards the region while engaging with China.

The signing of the Instruments of Accession and Extension to the Treaty of Amity and Cooperation (TAC) in Southeast Asia in July 2009 marked Washington's formal accession to the treaty and the refocusing of attention on Southeast Asia.[80] This was followed by the US emphasis on an imperative for linking Southeast Asia with the Indian Ocean in 2013 to form the "Indo-Pacific" – a critical maritime zone of operations, where 60 per cent of US naval ships were planned to be deployed by 2020.[81] These were clearly "visible signs of America's determination to sustain economic and politico-strategic roles in the broader region".[82] A substantial increase in the US military assistance to and an intelligence coordination with its ally the Philippines, which was engaged in a bitter territorial dispute with China in the South China Sea, also indicated its intention of remaining engaged with the region. Several other similar initiatives since the beginning of this decade pointed to its renewed focus on Southeast Asia (Table 2.1)

Table 2.1: Other US-Led Initiatives in Southeast Asia

Year	*Initiative*
2011	US-Indonesia Comprehensive Partnership
2011	Joint Vision for the Thai-US Defense Alliance
2012	Washington announces "Pivot to Asia"
2013	Trade and Investment Framework Agreement with Myanmar
2013	US-Vietnam Comprehensive Partnership
2013	Deployment of the first of four US Littoral Combat Ships in Singapore

Source: Collated from William T. Tow, "The US and Asia in 2013: From Primacy to Marginalisation?" *Asian Survey* 54 (1), January/February 2014: 20

A greater US presence in the region has significantly influenced China's policies towards Southeast Asia. During the last few years, greater US activism – like its "pivot to Asia" strategy – in China's periphery has resulted in intense strategic rivalry between the two major powers. Southeast Asian countries, as a result, have been pulled in opposite directions. Some countries of the region are eager on US leadership as they perceive President Xi as a "strong nationalist who will put China's interests, including its priorities regarding sovereignty, above all other considerations" and also believe that the Chinese leadership prefers "a weak ASEAN"[83] for increasing its bargaining power with the region. However, even with respect to the US it is interesting to note the dilemma often faced by the Southeast Asian countries in this regard. As mentioned earlier, disputes with China and concerns over its assertiveness do encourage some Southeast Asian countries to urge a greater presence of the US. At the same time, the inclination on part of these countries to offer more strategic space to the US is accompanied by their reluctance to allow the establishment of permanent military bases like Okinawa in Japan or the former Clark Air base in Philippines.[84] As a result, the US has been working on new and flexible arrangements like joint military exercises and stationing and docking arrangements that avoid whipping up nationalist sentiments in the region.[85]

While alignment and realignment (with the US or China) have dominated the foreign policy discourse of the Southeast Asian countries, their regional "position" on China, particularly with respect to the South China Sea, have, time and again, been split. This was evident during the ASEAN ministerial meeting at Phnom Penh in 2012, when the grouping failed to issue a joint communiqueì due to Cambodia's refusal to agree to an aggressive description of China. Thereafter in April 2016, China was again successful in reaching at a four-point consensus with Brunei, Cambodia and Laos underlining that territorial disputes in the South China Sea were "not an issue between China and ASEAN as whole",[86] thus successfully dividing the grouping. The same year in June, the ASEAN-China Special Foreign Ministers' Meeting in China was concluded without a joint press conference by the co-chairs of the meeting – China and Singapore – due to a lack of agreement on the South China Sea. It was alleged that following the meeting, Cambodia, Laos and Myanmar had forced the recall of the ASEAN joint press statement by withdrawing their support on the statement, under the pressure of Beijing, which was to be released separately by the host, China.[87] These occasions have not only flaunted China's ability to split the ASEAN to suit its national interests but have equally exposed the ASEAN's weakness when confronted with a powerful and assertive China.

While the future course of the US policy towards the region is uncertain, a low profile by Washington would allow China more strategic space and the opportunity of creating new alliances and partnerships. Philippines, a treaty ally of the United States since 1951, has already shown the tendency of cozying up to China even before Trump came to power.[88] The Filipino President Rodrigo Duterte, who took office in June 2016, has shown the resolve to chart a new course of foreign policy by distancing from Washington and inching closer to a partnership with Beijing, which might also include Moscow.[89] Malaysia also seems to be inching closer to China with the proposed "landmark" defence deal with China, underscoring a strategic shift away from the US.[90]

Beijing, though, is unlikely to pursue a strategy for engaging Southeast Asia that would be exclusive of the geostrategic implications of the US presence in the region. Xi Jinping's proposal for a "New Type of Great Power Relations" floated first during his visit to Washington in February 2012 reflects the main contours of the Chinese policy towards Southeast Asia, and Asia in general, in connection to the "China Dream" discussed earlier. According to strategic experts like Mohan Malik, the "New Type of Great Power Relations" seeks a US recognition of China's preeminence in Asia, while attempting to limit Washington's regional role and presence and relegate traditional US allies (especially Japan) to the sidelines.[91] Scholars like Wang Yi contrast the thought by arguing that Xi's new model seeks to avoid conflict while ensuring mutual benefit and a win-win situation for both the US and China while underscoring that China "never thought about pushing the US out of the [Asia-Pacific] region".[92] Nonetheless, the US reaction to the articulation of Xi Jinping's vision was clearly that of precipitate counterbalancing, as is obvious from the pronouncement of the "pivot to Asia" by the former US Secretary of State, Hillary Clinton soon after in July 2012. The strategy outlined Washington's plan "to lock in a substantially increased investment – diplomatic, economic, strategic, and otherwise – in the Asia-Pacific region",[93] and demonstrated its intent to remain involved with the Asian part of the Pacific.

While the strategy of the new US administration towards Southeast Asia is yet to assume clear dimensions, Washington is unlikely to disengage with the region, especially over the maritime resources and routes of the region that are the driving factors in this regard. Washington's substantial maritime presence in the region has been sustained and maintained since World War II.[94] The presence has enabled trade and economic exchanges between the US and Asia contributing to the former's global power status for decades. Despite being an extra regional power, the US has close relations with most countries in Southeast Asia. It has been a traditional ally of Thailand and the Philippines,[95] has close relations with Singapore[96] and Indonesia and diplomatic ties with Cambodia and Myanmar. Malaysia and the US are also close allies and diplomatic partners while a comprehensive partnership defines Hanoi's current relationship with Washington. Notwithstanding these associations, the rise of "new pivots" like China – states with a significant degree of influence over the security of the commons (the Seas) – and the declining influence of Japan has made the region a theatre for conflict. The US is concerned that a pivotal state like China with substantive military capability within the global commons will threaten its dominance in the Asia-Pacific. There is no reason why the concern should dissipate with a change in the US administration and therefore, the renewed focus on the region. The objectives behind the US strategy of balancing the region, given a resurgent China and enhancing its presence, was spelt out in the *Quadrennial Defense Review* (QDR) of 2014 as well.[97]

Washington's desire of not wanting to be marginalised in China's neighbourhood [or for that matter in any other part of the world] where China's economic outreach is significant, might, however, be impacted by other decisions of the US administration that might affect the region. A pertinent example is the withdrawal of the US from the Trans-Pacific Partnership (TPP). A US administration initiative connected to the "pivot to Asia" strategy that had the US and eleven other countries including four countries in Southeast Asia (Brunei, Malaysia, Singapore and Vietnam with the likelihood of Thailand and Philippines joining in future) has been severely dented in economic and strategic effectiveness following the US withdrawal and has been a major source of disappointment for US allies like Singapore. Prime Minister Lee during an interview stated that "I think this has put a dent in the degree to which people can be confident of America's policies", since the small island country had placed enormous strategic importance on the TPP.[98]

Indeed, such an action also creates doubts over whether the region will continue to witness a robust US public diplomacy through state visits, which had gathered rapid momentum during President Obama's administration. In 2014, President Obama visited Philippines and Malaysia and described the US-Philippine alliance as "ironclad" signalling a strong message to China while making clear Washington's commitment to the pivot.[99] The US President visited Myanmar too in 2014 to attend the East Asia Summit (EAS), after his earlier visit in 2012, demonstrating the extent to which Washington was wedded to rapprochement with Naypyidaw. Added to this, was an active public diplomacy that was in the form of upgraded military relations with Singapore, Philippines, Thailand, Vietnam, Malaysia, Indonesia and Brunei highlighting Washington's strategic priority of the region. As far as state visits are concerned, there is an indication that face-to-face diplomacy will continue to dominate US's external engagement with Southeast Asia even under Trump. The US Vice President Mike Pence's visit to Indonesia in early 2017 and the proposed Trump visit to the region for the US-ASEAN, the East Asian Summit (both in Philippines) and the APEC (in Vietnam) in 2017 underlines that the US administration cannot afford to abandon Southeast Asia and the region's criticality in Washington's foreign policy.

Though the region still seems critical for the current US administration, from the perspective of many countries in Southeast Asia, President Donald Trump's election has given rise to scepticism and speculation. The absence of a clear policy agenda and the vacillating posture on part of the Trump administration does make the region vulnerable and undermined. Nonetheless, the initial uncertainty following Trump's pronouncement of an "America first" world view has gradually given way to a more optimistic perception based on the fact that since 1945 Washington has never really disengaged with the region. In fact, the Singapore government has been quite optimistic with the PM being confident that despite Washington's pulling out of the TPP, it is unlikely to withdraw from Asia. The regional sentiment has been further buoyed with the US President and Japanese Prime Minister hailing the US-Japan alliance as the cornerstone for regional peace in February 2017 at their joint press conference in the White House. The alliance has bolstered the primacy of realpolitik and national interests, partly reassuring the Southeast Asian countries that the power balance would be maintained in the region with no direct threat to their interests. The special US-ASEAN Foreign Ministers meeting held in Washington in early May 2017 between the US Secretary of State Rex Tillerson and the ASEAN Foreign Ministers, further reassured the region that the US leadership would continue to remain engaged with the region.[100] The meeting witnessed the US administration reinforcing its strategic partnership while committing to address the challenges faced by the region, including the South China Sea dispute and North Korea's missile programme.

While the US has loomed large in Chinese strategic thinking on Southeast Asia, India has not had such specific concerns. However, with complicated dynamics shaping the regional order, China is gradually noticing India's growing engagement with Southeast Asia. Perceived as an extra-regional power in the region by China, India's defence deal with Vietnam[101] and its gradual involvement in the South China Sea dispute[102] might prove challenging for Beijing: "Instead of unnecessary entanglements with China over the South China Sea debate during Wang's visit", a piece in the *Global Times* declared, "India must create a good atmosphere for economic cooperation, including the reduction of tariffs...amid the ongoing free trade talks".[103] This is interesting since China's increasing engagement with South Asia, or more specifically in India's periphery, is viewed with as much, if not greater suspicion by India. Countries from Southeast Asia, though, have preferred the presence of both Washington and New Delhi as also Australia and Japan, for achieving their economic and strategic goals. At the same time, they have been careful about not jeopardising relations with China, which is evident from China's active participation in the ASEAN and ASEAN-centric regional associations.

* * *

Southeast Asia's geopolitical significance has been enhanced by the US-China rivalry, which is produced by a common urge to control its maritime space that not only contains untapped energy and natural resources, but is also the conduit to huge cross-continental trade between Asia, the Americas and Europe. The region, as a result, is prominent in strategic calculus of several extra-regional actors like

China, Australia, Japan, the US and India. Apart from the US, the region is a geographical periphery, or part of the extended neighbourhood of all the other extra-regional actors mentioned, thereby making it significant in all of the latter countries' foreign policies. The US interest in the region, apart from the generic issue of control over maritime resources, stems from its interest in counterbalancing China – an interest, which is becoming increasingly prominent in India's strategic vision of the region as well.

While many countries in Southeast Asia have historical links with India and China, strategic interests, primarily produced by China's rise and the resultant assertiveness, have led them to develop stronger relationships with other non-Chinese extra-regional actors including the US. These proclivities have complicated the political and military environment of the region where great power relations have shifted from an American preponderance to a relationship based on China's rise and a US "pivot"[104] with India, Australia and Japan playing "marginal roles". All these complexities have made image-building efforts by India and China both critical and a challenge to overcome. In addition, a US administration led by Donald Trump is already adding to the complexities. The new administration might alter the relations further depending on whether the US "pivot" to Asia loses traction altogether, or paves the way for more US military activism in the region, unleashing an adverse power play and concomitant instability in the regional order. In fact, Trump's excessive focus on North Korea's nuclear weapons programme coupled with his decision to suspend naval patrols of islands and reefs claimed by China have been translated by the Southeast Asian countries as the administration's unwillingness to challenge China's territorial claims. This often vacillating Trump approach is seen as jeopardising its long-term economic and security partners in the region[105] which have been looking towards the US for direction and leadership faced with Beijing's increased activism in the region. This has also led the Vietnam Prime Minister Nguyen Xuan Phuc wanting to visit the US – the first Southeast Asian leader to visit Washington – to ascertain the "US policy and strategy toward the South China Sea and China's activities there, particularly at a time when Washington is looking to Beijing to rein in North Korea's nuclear and missile programs".[106] In the meantime,

Australia is already showing an interest to play a more active leadership role in Southeast Asia while new groupings like Australia-Indonesia-Japan may be expected to "offset potentially eroding US support" and prevent the risk of Southeast Asian countries realigning with China.[107] Such alignments and cooperation are already on the cards. According to a report in February 2017, the Indonesian President has plans to discuss the prospect of joint patrols with Australia in the South China Sea.[108]

Actions like the US pulling out of the TPP has also confused the ASEAN regarding the nature of the strategic balance in the region with China not showing signs of any compromise on sovereignty issues on the South China Sea and instead, upgrading its military hardware. The US administration's ambiguous posturing including an earlier assertion by President Trump during his election campaign of larger military deployment in the South China Sea for countering China's "adventurism" and later seeking China's assistance for reining in North Korea along with the focus on "America first" and little mention of the region in foreign policy statements after his election, are disturbing for the region. The US ambiguity, as some countries in Southeast Asia would anticipate, might encourage China to push its national interest projects like the OBOR more aggressively in the region. Territorial disputes too might heighten, leading to greater geopolitical risks. Beijing is well-placed to utilise the current situation by creating a zero-sum "with us or without us" game matrix compelling Southeast Asian countries to choose between the US – which looks more uncertain of its role or maybe more disengaged with the region than before – and China, which has been and will be the most important player in Asia. The manifestation of such a possibility is already visible in the region through shifting alliances, as demonstrated by Philippines, Malaysia and even Cambodia.

Notwithstanding Southeast Asia's economic linkages with China, its overarching concern over Beijing's political, military and territorial ambitions have enhanced in recent years, particularly on sovereignty issues in the South China Sea. In many respects, as discussed earlier, this creates strategic opportunities for India in the region. Though still a marginal player compared with the strategic clout of other extra-regional actors, New Delhi's recent foreign policy activism with respect to the region is noticeable, especially through initiatives like the "Act East" policy. While both India and China are determined to strengthen relations with the Southeast Asian countries, their successes will depend to a great extent on the images they project in this regard. For India, the challenge is to keep up the enthusiasm for forging stronger ties with the region while improving its political and economic perceptions. For China, on the other hand, the challenge is to manage its "assertiveness" while working on more confidence-building-measures (CBMs). The next two chapters will examine the soft power tools being applied by India and China for improving their "images" alongside efforts to strengthen engagement with the region for pursuing "enlightened" national interests.[109]

ENDNOTES

1. Lustick, 'The absence of Middle Eastern Great Powers': 653-83
2. Ibid
3. Minxin, 'Think again: Asia's rise'
4. Quah, 'World's center of economic gravity shifts east'
5. The concept of Southeast Asia as a geopolitical region is a product of World War II, when the newly independent nation states of Southeast Asia emerged, with foreign policymakers and scholars of international relations beginning to study this group of countries as an international region. As rightly pointed out, 'the external awareness of a Southeast Asian region at this early point was primarily a product of its geostrategic position in the Cold War'. These states can be defined as being politically, ethnically and religiously diverse, with economic inequalities. For details see Weatherbee, *International Relations in Southeast Asia*: 7, 9
6. The ASEAN was founded on August 8, 1967 by Indonesia, Malaysia, Singapore, Thailand and Philippines for promoting mutual economic growth, social progress and cultural development. Later Brunei joined the Group in 1984 and Vietnam in 1995. Laos and Burma became its members in 1997 and Cambodia in 1999.
7. Trump had indicated several times during his speeches to the run-up to the election that he was in favour of withdrawing troops from Japan and South Korea, thereby confusing the region. Trump's plan had raised serious concerns in many Southeast Asian countries which feared that this 'new' American strategy, if put to work, would not only embolden China but lead to an arms/nuclear race in the region.
8. The Australian concern that the archipelago of Southeast Asia maybe the route by which the extra-regional powers might pose security threats to Australia, has made it engage with the region. The *Defense White Paper 2013* has taken this into account. In a marked departure from its predecessors, this paper mentioned that

Southeast Asia "looms as the new player on Australia's strategic landscape". Southeast Asia is "central" to Australia's concerns about the Indo-Pacific with Australian security interests "intertwined" with Indonesia.

9. 'Hand in Hand'
10. Panikkar, *The future of Southeast Asia, an Indian view*
11. Sen Gupta, 'India in the Twenty-First Century': 309
12. India has the second longest border, both in terms of land and maritime together, with Myanmar. India's Andaman and Nicobar Islands share a maritime border with Thailand along the Andaman Sea.
13. Brewster, 'India's engagements with Southeast Asia: Singapore, Vietnam and Indonesia'
14. According to the former Indian Foreign Secretary Nirupama Rao, the "core" Indo-Pacific is a "stretch of oceanic space that links the Indian and Pacific Oceans" and is a significant geo-economic arena for trade flows. For details see Rao, 'America's "Asian pivot": The view from India'
15. *Defence White Paper* 2016, Australian Government
16. Tharoor, *Pax Indica*
17. Malone, 'Soft Power in India's foreign policy'
18. Leur, 'On early Asian trade'
19. Coedes, *The Indianised states of Southeast Asia*: 34
20. Tharoor: 184
21. Ibid
22. Many theories abound regarding the invasion. According to Nilkanta Sastri, the invasion could have been because Srivijaya attempted to obstruct the Chola trade with the East (especially China). It could also have been due to King Rajendra Chola's desire to extend the reach of the Digvijaya empire across the seas. See Sastri: 220
23. The Australia *Defense White Paper* 2016 mentions India as a "key partner" and looks to "mature and deepen practical engagement" with India, along with Indonesia, Japan, South Korea, New Zealand and China. For details see Hall, 'India in Australia's 2016 Defence White Paper'
24. Apart from the Sea, the other three global commons are air, space and cyberspace.
25. Bajpai, *India's Foreign Policy: A Reader*: 17
26. Purushothaman, 'India's strategic dimensions in Malacca Strait'
27. Mohan, 'Is India an East Asian power? Explaining New Delhi's security politics in the Western Pacific'
28. Price, Gareth, 'India's policy towards Burma'
29. Iyengar, 'India is using its military incursions into Burma to send a message to other countries'
30. Roche, 'India, with an eye on ASEAN, looks to deepen ties with Malaysia'
31. Ibid
32. Sharma, 'Why Indonesia is important for India'
33. Veeramalla, 'Jokowi's global maritime axis doctrine key to Indonesia's future'
34. Price, 'India's policy towards Burma'
35. 'USA knew there was mega deposits of oil in Vietnam in the fifties'

36. Roche, 'India, with an eye on ASEAN, looks to deepen ties with Malaysia'
37. Kumar, 'Why India-Vietnam ties are important?'
38. Vietnam looks to increase its weapons exports to US$2 billion in the coming years from India. See Clark, 'Why China should fear India's arms sales to Vietnam (Think South China Sea)'
39. *India-Philippines Relations*
40. *India-Singapore relations*
41. 'If Only Singaporeans stopped to think'
42. India and Malaysia have also been participating in the MILAN naval exercises – first held in 1995 – along with Bangladesh, Sri Lanka, Indonesia, Singapore and Thailand – aiming to strengthen cooperation among the navies in the region.
43. Joint Statement on a strategic partnership by the Prime Ministers of the Republic of India and the Republic of Singapore 'Renewed Sprite and New Energy'
44. Statement by India and Indonesia on maritime cooperation
45. 'ASEAN, India to boost cultural cooperation and linkages'
46. As of May 2017, all the Southeast Asian countries seem quite enthusiastic to partner China over the OBOR. It is only India which has kept away from the initiative over sovereignty issues.
47. The US enthusiasm was evident in the Joint Strategic Vision in welcoming India's bid for membership of the APEC: '...the United States welcomes India's interest in joining the Asia-Pacific Economic Cooperation forum, as the Indian economy is a dynamic part of the Asian economy'. See Palit, 'India's bid for APEC membership: Trade policy is the stumbling block'
48. Beri, 'Maritime Security'
49. Malaysia is one of the largest countries in the region and with a large Indian diaspora.
50. The Make in India initiative was launched in September 2014 by the Indian Prime Minister Narendra Modi to make India a global manufacturing hub and by encouraging internatonal and domestic companies to manufacture in India.
51. 'Modi in Singapore: PM praises Indian diaspora'
52. Swaine, 'Chinese view and Commentary on Periphery Diplomacy'
53. Ibid
54. Thayer, *The Borderlands of Southeast Asia: Geopolitics, Terrorism, and Globalisation*: 236
55. Min, 'Balancing in a hierarchical system: Pre-colonial Southeast Asia and the tribute system': 227-56
56. In the Chinese Tribute System, the imperial court was at the Centre with the surrounding states as its dependents. Without the institution of 'sovereignty', it was a China-centred system whereby the tribute system conceptually represented concentric circles around the Forbidden City where the Emperor held his court and the tributary states were the radiation of the centre with only a difference in distance. For details see Qin, 'Why is there no Chinese International Theory'
57. Qin, 'Why is there no Chinese International Theory'
58. *Tianxia's* roots go back to philosophical texts as early as the Zhou period (1046–221 BCE) dictated by Confucian norms of hierarchy and morality which deeply

influenced the concept of *Tianxia*, which remained a powerful influence through China's dynastic history. For details see Rigby, 'Tianxia'

59. Zhang Feng, 'The Tianxia system: world order in a Chinese utopia'
60. Rigby
61. Beijing's assistance was sought by the European powers to end the Indochina War.
62. China's attempt to gain regional preeminence was thwarted by the War.
63. Storey, *Southeast Asia and the rise of China*: 4
64. Arase, 'China's Two Silk Roads initiative: What it means for Southeast Asia'
65. Zhao, 'China's One Belt One Road: An overview of the debate'
66. Arase
67. 'President vows to bring benefits to people in realising "Chinese Dream"'
68. 'Deepening reform and upgrading China'
69. The domestic discussion of China's rise began in 1995. China's 'peaceful rise' grew for allaying concerns about the 'China threat'. It was perceived as a concept that negates the use of force and was expected to impact the international system in a positive way, as argued by Meng Yangqing.
70. 'China Focus: Chinese premier reaffirms road of peaceful development'
71. 'Xi advocates efforts to boost China's maritime power'
72. 'President Xi's remarks on South China Sea issue'
73. 'More "agile fleets needed" to tackle sea challenges'
74. Beng, 'China President Xi dismisses Hague arbitration on South China Sea but says "committed to peace"'
75. Kerrey, Manning, 'The United States and Southeast Asia: A policy agenda for the new administration'
76. Ibid
77. The Asian Infrastructure Investment Bank (AIIB), one of the institutions created by Beijing, is what many consider an attempt by the Chinese leadership to create a Sino-centric financial system to rival the Western dominated institutions set up after the Second World War.
78. Johnson, 'Decoding China's emerging "Great Power" strategy in Asia'
79. Political Scientist Randall Schweller points out how an established power deals with a rising power. According to him, the treatment is dependent on whether the rising power is risk-acceptant or risk-averse power. While a risk-acceptance power will be dealt with by balancing and deterrence (China in this case), risk-averse powers (like India) will see less engagement given that these powers pose no challenge and are mostly status quo powers. For details see Schweller, 'Managing the Rise of Great Powers'
80. The 9/11 and later Afghanistan had grabbed Washington's attention during the time.
81. 'A Cooperative Strategy for 21st century Sea Power'
82. Tow, 'The US and Asia in 2013: From Primacy to Marginalisation?': 20
83. Johnson, 'Decoding China's emerging 'Great Power' strategy in Asia'
84. Washington had to pull off its military base from the Philippines in 1991.
85. Zenn, 'US presence evolves in Southeast Asia'

86. Chanborey, 'The South China Sea and ASEAN unity: A Cambodian Perspective'
87. Ibid
88. Sometime during September 2016, Duterte had announced the ceasing of maritime cooperation with the US reflecting his anger at the American criticism of human rights abuses in the Philippines after he launched a drug war that killed many.
89. Perlez, 'Rodrigo Duterte gets closer to China, and the neighbours notice,
90. 'Malaysia strategic shift towards China in a setback to US'
91. Malik, 'China and strategic imbalance'
92. Wang Yi, 'Toward a new model of major-country relations between China and the United States'
93. Clinton, 'America's Pacific Century'
94. Denmark, 'Asia's security and the contested global commons': 170
95. The US provides Philippine s and Tailand non-NATO military alliance (NNMA) status.
96. Singapore is expanding defence cooperation arrangements with Washington.
97. *Quadrennial Defense Review*, 2014
98. 'Singapore: US withdrawal from trade pact hurts confidence - PM Hsien Loong'
99. Moss, 'Obama visit signals progress for Asia "Pivot"'
100. 'Secretary Tillerson Meets With the Foreign Ministers of the Association of Southeast Asian Nations'
101. India's decision to provide Vietnam with Akash surface-to-air missile systems mainly to act as a deterrent to any possible aggression against Vietnam, disturbs China. For details see 'Indian arms sale to Hanoi disturbing if aimed at China'
102. The Indo-US Joint Statement in 2014 mentioned the situation in the South China Sea for the first time.
103. China's Foreign Minister visited India in August 2016 to discuss India's candidature for the exclusive Nuclear Suppliers Group which it had previously blocked. For details see Singh, 'Why India's South China Sea stand matters'
104. Weatherbee, *International Relations in Southeast Asia*: 334
105. 'Trump's mixed signals on S China Sea worry Asia': 45
106. Jennings, 'Vietnam takes Asia lead in figuring out Trump policy on South China Sea'
107. Townshend, 'America First: US Asia policy under President Trump'
108. 'Indonesia to raise prospect of joint patrols with Australia in South China Sea: report'
109. In international diplomacy, 'enlightened' national interest is arguably the recognition that the narrow pursuit of self-interest in an interdependent world can lead to suboptimal policy outcomes for selfish pursuit of national ambitions. Rather, the objective of the government should be to pursue policies for the 'common good' instead.

3

India-Southeast Asia: Cooperation Key to "Asian Century"

The speech by the then External Affairs Minister, Pranab Mukherjee, in November 2006[1] that "India's foreign policy today looks at India's environment in expanding circles...starting with the immediate neighbourhood...moving on to...the extended neighbourhood" not only indicated the extent to which India was ready to engage the region but also underlined the leadership's enthusiasm to alter definitions of the "neighbourhood"[2] in keeping with the changing dynamics at the global as well as at the regional systemic. The former Defence Minister Manohar Parrikar's peroration a decade later at the annual Shangri la Dialogue of Defence Ministers in Singapore in June 2016 that "For India, located as we are at the centre of the Asian landmass astride the Indian Ocean, any reference to Asia implies its fullest geography ranging from the Suez to the shores of the Pacific" highlighted the expanding boundaries of India's neighbourhood and emerging security concerns for India's foreign policy with China making its presence felt in the Indian Ocean. The Chinese Navy's sustained operations in the Gulf of Aden since 2008 and its acquisition of a military base in Djibouti communicates its belligerent tendency, while Beijing's ambitious OBOR plans make New Delhi uncomfortable, thus making engagement of Southeast Asia and the Asia-Pacific countries like Australia and Japan critical in New Delhi's foreign policy for the region.

Various Indian governments, whether led by the Congress or the Bharatiya Janata Party (BJP), over the years, have been displaying considerable maturity in cultivating Southeast Asia by emphasising "highest priority to its relationship with ASEAN".[3] But the quality of India's engagement with the region falls short of robust levels. Added to this is New Delhi's policy inertia and preoccupation with domestic policies that have constrained India from pursuing an active foreign policy for the region. Nonetheless, given Southeast Asia's centrality in the regional architecture and New Delhi's eagerness to play a larger role beyond its immediate neighbourhood (South Asia),[4] India has gradually enhanced engagement with the region. However, it is important to note that though some individual countries figure more prominently in India's larger strategic vision, the region as a whole may not necessarily be the top priority for New Delhi. This tendency is largely because of India's economic and strategic priorities and also partly because its immediate foreign policy concerns have much to do with its national security rather than a broader regional strategy.[5]

As India has grown economically, its engagement strategy with neighbours has also become deeper and more intense, making image-building critical in forging partnerships. India's regional image has not been particularly positive in its neighborhood, making the process of image-building challenging. While it was idealism riding on high moral grounds that drove Indian foreign policy post-independence and to a great extent conditioned India's image, in more recent years, particularly after the economic reforms, there has been a gradual progression based on pragmatism. However, India's image continues to suffer from incoherence, clarity and unpredictability that influences regional perceptions of India. To play a big power role India needs to work on its image and transform it to communicate confidence, activism, positive intent, responsible behaviour and economic stability for the regional players to take notice of. The last few leaderships have attempted to resurrect India's image and infuse more energy into it to indicate that it is ready to play a bigger role not only in regional affairs but globally as well. It is important for "middle" or "emerging" powers like India to be risk-acceptant as opposed to being risk-averse since the latter are considered "timid" and less likely to challenge the status quo, providing relatively lesser incentives for other countries to engage them as opposed to large powers.[6]

The Look East Policy (LEP), which aimed to enhance India's economic integration in particular with Southeast Asia, also targeted to develop political contacts and forge security cooperation with countries from the region. Officially defined and articulated by Prime Minister PV Narasimha Rao in 1994,[7] it was rigorously pursued by the administrations of Atal Bihari Vajpayee and Manmohan Singh.[8] The Modi government, which came to power in 2014, decided to further push the initiative, in keeping with its larger geostrategic agenda, by upgrading the LEP into the "Act East Policy" (AEP). While the LEP was partly initiated for seeking India's leadership role in Southeast Asia,[9] it highlighted New Delhi's choice for regionalism, which now encompasses a larger geographical expanse.

Has India been able to constructively engage the region since the LEP was introduced in 1994? To what extent have forums like the ASEAN played an enabling role for India to deepen its engagement with the region? These are some of the questions this chapter will seek to address while discussing the other soft power tools like cultural initiatives as well as selective economic tools that India has been employing to strengthen its ties with Southeast Asia.

India's Tryst with Regionalism[10]: Look East Policy (LEP) and Act East Policy (AEP)

Barry Buzan and O. Waever in *Regions and Power* argue that with decolonisation the "regional" level has not only gained autonomy but also greater prominence in global politics, thereby attesting to the emergence of a "post-hegemonic" international system. The end of the Cold War further bolstered regional security dynamics. According to Rosecrance, the new evolving international order put "an end to the bipolar cleavage" leading "to a restoration of regional sovereignty" and to the establishment of "several regional powers dominating their geographical areas".[11] The end of the bipolar world impacted dynamics in Asia as well with India looking for more strategic space within the region. However, this was also the time when the US began readjusting its foreign policy trajectory towards Asia, including Southeast Asia, specifically.[12]

Faced with a new "post-hegemonic" international system reflecting greater salience of the "region" coupled with new regional security dynamics in its Asian neighbourhood, India's power ambitions compelled it to engage with the region[13] while at the same time encouraging an image make-over. Regionalism also began evolving as a tool for meeting New Delhi's larger national interests. As constructivists have suggested and as it has been clear with respect to both India and China, they are employing regionalism to promote specific goals. This section looks at India's use of regionalism to stress cooperation and partnership with the region for meeting its larger national interests: both strategic and economic. While cooperation and partnership with several of Southeast Asian countries have been underway, India's policy initiatives towards the region still lack depth and variety compared with similar initiatives by China.

India's need to reconnect with Southeast Asia[14] led India to join the ASEAN as a sectoral dialogue partner[15] in 1992, thereby securing its place in the ASEAN-centric regional architecture of the Asia-Pacific, subsequently paving the way for launching the LEP in 1994 and a full dialogue partner the following year. But the LEP has suffered from limitations. Many argue that the LEP not only "remains limited in its impact because its domestic drivers have remained largely untapped",[16] but also because there is a disconnect between what India aspires from the LEP and what the Southeast Asian countries expect from India and its actions through this initiative.

New Delhi's admission into the ASEAN was not only seen as a signal of its acceptance by the ASEAN countries alone but also by Australia and Japan[17] – two major powers in the region – of India's role and position in the Asia-Pacific region. However, the term LEP figured in India's *Annual Report* of the Ministry of External Affairs (MEA) for the first time in 1996 when India was admitted into the ASEAN Regional Forum (ARF) (Table 3.1) – perhaps indicating that LEP till 1996 wasn't a sufficiently high priority within India's foreign policy establishment itself. Given that one of the instrumental factors in the launch of the LEP was India's decision to integrate deeper with the regional economies, it was perhaps also natural for the Southeast Asian countries to wait and watch India's economic liberalisation and performance.[18] Indeed, India's decision to adopt outward-oriented economic policies made it an attractive and hitherto unexploited location for pursuing business opportunities for Southeast Asia encouraging dynamic economies like Singapore, Malaysia and Thailand, to look more closely at India.

Table 3.1: India's Major Engagement Initiatives with Southeast Asia (1991-2012)

Year	*Initiatives*
1991	LEP initiated
1992	India joins ASEAN as a sectoral dialogue partner
1993	Several high-level visits undertaken to Southeast Asian countries (Thailand, Myanmar, Vietnam)
1994	Formal launch of LEP. PM Rao visited Singapore where he delivered the *Singapore Lecture*. The *Lecture* while underlining the new-found confidence and strength of a forum like ASEAN also announced the government's intent to play a larger role in Southeast Asia. It also highlighted India's "open economy" and the Indian people enthused about "the benefits of exposure to the outside world"
1995	Upgraded to a Full Dialogue Partnership at the Fifth ASEAN Summit in Bangkok
1996	India admitted into the ARF
2002	Upgraded to a Summit Level Partnership
2003	India and ASEAN signed the Framework Agreement on Comprehensive Economic Cooperation, leading to the creation of a Free Trade Area (FTA) by the year 2011 and India's accession to the Treaty of Amity and Cooperation in Southeast Asia
2004	ASEAN-India Partnership for Peace, Progress and Shared Prosperity
2005	India became a founding member of the East Asia Summit (EAS)
2009	India signed the ASEAN–India FTA with the 10 members of ASEAN
2012	India-ASEAN relations upgraded to strategic partnership

Source: Compiled by the author from various sources

Through the LEP India began its tryst with regionalism, which assumed relevance and significance in India's foreign policymaking overtime. While trade and investment largely have remained the focus of its engagement strategy, people-to-people communication through tourism and cultural exchanges have also evolved as thrust areas for deepening collaboration between India and the ASEAN, as well as between India and important Asia-Pacific countries like Australia and Japan. LEP represents the beginning of a new policy/strategic thinking on the part of the Indian leadership for whom domestic economic reforms not only led to change in perceptions about India's role in the larger global and regional context, but also imparted dynamism to economic cooperation. However, if bilateral trade is used for measuring the success of economic engagement, trade with Southeast Asia is yet to acquire the significance that trade with Europe and some other parts of the world have for India.[19]

The degree of economic engagement between India and the region's countries has not been uniform. Economic engagements with larger economies like Indonesia and Philippines as well as economically backward economies like Cambodia and Laos has been much less than those with Singapore, Malaysia and Thailand. Also, as noted by economist Amitendu Palit, the "Indian producers are hardly prominent in regional value chains (RVCs) running through ASEAN. This might be due to relatively lower utilisation of the regional FTAs".[20] The heterogeneous quality of economic engagement has been accompanied by a distinct ambiguity in the LEP. With China's gradual ascent and growing influence in the Asia-Pacific, the LEP was seen as a stepping stone for expanding Indian influence in Southeast Asia and possibly beyond. However, the objective has remained largely unfulfilled. India's strategic influence over the region remains less than what its power would entail at a time when the region is experiencing more and more complications in its security environment: "Southeast Asia is locked into a growing web of economic and physical interconnectivity with China, with its security needs mostly provided by the United States".[21]

India and ASEAN

The LEP and India's improving economic fundamentals and bright prospects enabled it to become a part of the ASEAN dialogue mechanism and participate in several ASEAN-centric forums like the East Asia Summit (EAS), ASEAN Regional Forum (ARF), the ASEAN Defence Ministers' Meeting Plus (ADMM+), and the Expanded ASEAN Maritime Forum (EAMF). The LEP assisted India's interface with Japan and Australia as well, apart from building closer ties with the Southeast Asian countries. Economic cooperation being the hallmark of the ASEAN framework, forums like the EAS and the ARF seek to strengthen India's economic engagement with the ASEAN member countries while trying to progress on overall regional economic development. The ASEAN+6 is another economic initiative launched in 2008 as a step towards the Asian Economic Community including India.[22] India's economic engagement has increased through the Free Trade Agreements (FTAs) it has entered into with the ASEAN on goods and services. The India-ASEAN FTA is one of the five ASEAN+1 FTAs, the others being ASEAN's FTAs with China, Japan, Korea and Australia and New Zealand. These ASEAN+1 FTAs have become the common point for the growth of the Regional Comprehensive Economic Partnership (RCEP) pact, another major FTA being negotiated by the ten ASEAN countries and the six ASEAN FTA partners (including Australia, China, India, Japan, South Korea and New Zealand).

With the region's uncertain internal dynamics, defence cooperation has become an increasingly complex challenge for the ASEAN and its neighbours. Through the ADMM+ forums, CBMs have consequently emerged as a priority in this respect.[23] With its primary objective to build and sustain confidence between military and civilian defence officials and develop the practice of working together on transnational security issues, the ADMM+ tries to "engage and reassure China, rather than isolate it".[24] Notwithstanding several CBMs in place, a collision between the ASEAN member countries and China on several issues continues to cast a shadow on the region. In addition, given the Trump administrations's shifting priorities and vacillating foreign policy postures as discussed in the last chapter, it is not clear how the dynamics in the region will shape up with the situation getting more challenging for the region and its neighbours including India. In this context, forums such as the EAMF, aiming to enhance maritime cooperation and build trust in the region, become critical for India.

The concerns over maritime security and cooperation for India are now prominent in the Indian Ocean Region (IOR) given China's increasing footprint in South Asia[25] and its ambitious BRI connectivity plan. It is imperative for New Delhi to strengthen its navy in an attempt to restore India's sphere of influence while constructively engaging and safeguarding the IOR. In line with such efforts, striking new maritime partnerships also become important, driving home the significance of the India-Japan maritime cooperation. During the third annual meeting between the Indian and Japanese Prime Ministers in November 2016, a Joint Statement was issued on the Indo-Pacific region highlighting its significance for the two partners. The "idea" of the Indo-Pacific will see an enhanced naval cooperation not only between India and Japan but with Australia as well. Closely linked to this will be India and Japan's efforts for increasing connectivity in the IOR. In fact, corridors to connect Asia and Africa through the Indian Ocean (Asia-Africa Growth Corridor) is already on the cards. The Joint Statement in 2016 between Prime Ministers Abe and Modi called for such a continental initiative which could be a significant strategic counter to China's Maritime Silk Road.[26]

India and Japan are equally keen to cultivate Southeast Asia, given that they have a common interest in ensuring a continued access to the SLOCs through this region; thus, their strategic and maritime interests coinciding in the process. Many Asian scholars are even suggesting that "one potential candidate to spearhead an eventual trilateral maritime partnership between India, Japan and ASEAN would be Singapore, a geostrategically well-located small island-city state that is heavily dependent on SLOC security for its national survival and prosperity".[27] In the meantime, the India-Malaysia naval cooperation is also picking up though it is largely in the form of training interactions and exchange of goodwill visits. India's naval cooperation with Vietnam is also an equally important maritime partnership. Such cooperation with a Southeast Asian country which has disputes with China over the South China Sea is an indication that New Delhi is ready to engage each major country in Southeast Asia, irrespective of its complex relationship with China "on its own merit". According to Raja Mohan, "this translates into a twin track Indian diplomacy in Asia: build on the new economic possibilities with China but don't allow it to define the limits of India's partnership with Japan and Vietnam".[28] The strategy aims to work with the notion "that our commons – ocean, space, and cyber – remain avenues of shared prosperity" rather than "new theatres of contests", as reiterated by the Indian Prime Minister Modi at the Shangri la, Singapore in November 2015.[29]

Apart from ensuring peace and security in the IOR and naval cooperation with its neighbours, projecting naval power has increasingly become visible in India's external engagement. The power projections have been in keeping with its larger global and regional ambitions. This naval dominance was showcased during the 2014-15 period when the Indian Navy sent frontline warships to countries from the Western Pacific in the East to those on the West coast of South Adriatic showing the Indian flag in almost all the major ports while interacting with friendly navies in the region,[30] thus reflecting new energy and intent for furthering engagement and projecting its blue water strength. These exercises have been employed by India to partner countries like Australia which are also committed to strengthening their naval capabilities in Asia. Apart from naval exercises with other countries, government-to-government initiatives like the India-ASEAN Delhi Dialogue,[31] organised by the MEA, are also contributing to a greater engagement with the region and exploring the possibility of widening the scope of engagement beyond economics. Such platforms are also used to announce policies and reflect new directions in foreign policy. The Delhi Dialogue – IX, held in New Delhi in early July 2017, was employed by the Indian leadership to announce its intent to invite the leaders of the 10 ASEAN countries for the Republic Day parade and celebrations in 2018, while highlighting 25 years of dialogue partnership, 15 years of summit-level interaction, and five years of strategic partnership, through a wide range of activities.[32] This once again reflects the Indian leadership's intent for deepening engagement with the region, particularly at a time when India and China were involved in a stand-off over the Bhutanese Doklam region.

The Modi government's efforts to use regionalism as a foreign policy tool is in line with India's AEP. Indeed, the use of regional organisations like the ASEAN to reiterate collaboration and partnership with India's extended neighbourhood, apart from communicating messages that would have a bearing on its national interest, has evolved as the new mantra. It was tactical on the part of Prime Minister Modi to announce AEP at the ASEAN summit in Myanmar's capital

Naypyidaw in 2014, thus signifying the importance India attaches to Myanmar – the only country in the region that shares land and sea borders with India and serves as a gateway to Southeast Asia. Announced as an upgraded LEP, the AEP not only indicates a more action-oriented policy towards ASEAN, but communicates the leaderships' intent to engage Oceania and East Asia, and the current government's efforts to maintain "continuity" in India's engagement policy with its neighbours.

While announcing the AEP, Prime Minister Modi also highlighted New Delhi's aim to further strengthen economic relations with the ASEAN countries including establishing a Special Purpose Vehicle (SPV) for setting up manufacturing hubs in the CLMV countries (Cambodia, Laos, Myanmar, Vietnam) for facilitating private Indian investments in the region[33] while inviting the Southeast Asian countries to be part of India's economic transformation. It is interesting to note that the Indian government has also been focusing on connectivity projects as a tool for reaching out to its neighbours, pretty similar to China. But the Indian initiatives remain slower and smaller compared with China, underscoring China's greater capabilities in employing connectivity for engaging neighbours through mega-projects like the BRI.[34] Nonetheless, the AEP marks a new phase of India's efforts to engage deeper with Southeast Asia and regional partners. It also reflects India's maritime ambition by working closely with regional partners to help ensure the freedom of navigation in Asia's regional waters.

India's engagement with Australia and Japan has also expanded since the 1990s with economics being the main driver of the engagement following India's economic liberalisation. It is noteworthy that a closer engagement with the ASEAN, Australia and Japan has helped India to alter its Cold War image as an ally of the former Soviet Union and has instead helped to project its willingness to partner other countries in the region in an effort to achieve its national objectives and strive for common development, similar to China. In this regard, the new image-building effort has extended to Southeast Asia and beyond, particularly Australia and Japan, which are key actors in the APEC framework. The Southeast Asian countries, especially during the 1980s, and even Japan were apprehensive of India's image given

New Delhi's military ambitions, rising defence budget and increasing footprint of its navy during the time.[35] The LEP and engagement with the ASEAN has been critical for allaying misconceptions about India and for building closer relationships with the regional partners. India's rising economic growth trajectory since the 1990s and good economic prospects have encouraged Japan and Australia to look at it more closely, in a manner similar to the Southeast Asian countries. Successive Indian governments, irrespective of the political party running the governments, have emphasised improving relations with the Asian neighbours. For example, while PV Narasimha Rao launched the LEP, Yashwant Sinha, Minister of External Affairs (2002-2004), during the NDA government led by Prime Minister Vajpayee, augmented the broader objectives of "India's Look East Policy in the new millennium", by indicating a Phase II "characterised by an expanded definition of "East" extending from Australia to China and East Asia with ASEAN as its core".[36] The Modi government, by launching the AEP, has continued the earlier policy and added more substance to it by including connectivity and economic infrastructure-building plans within its fold. However, there is a need to include technology transfer, civilian nuclear cooperation, defence and innovation into its current ambit as well.[37]

Driven primarily by economics, Phase II also highlighted the emphasis on security including collaborative efforts to protect the SLOCs and fighting terrorism in which the cooperation of countries like Australia and Japan are essential for India. Both are active democracies with political systems and institutions similar to India and are also in this sense its "natural" partners. Prime Minister Modi's AEP is a further vindication of India's calibrated approach to deepen its association with the extended neighbourhood, including APEC members like Australia and Japan, for promoting regional security and heralding an Asia-Pacific Century. India's expanding maritime interest has further led it to partner Australia with the latter being prominent in both the Indian Ocean Naval Symposium (IONS) and the Indian Ocean Rim Association (IORA) – the two multilateral institutions in which New Delhi has a substantial stake.

Other Sub-Regional Initiatives

Apart from the ASEAN-centric forums, India has correspondingly been engaged in cross-regional cooperation through initiatives like the Bay of Bengal Initiative for Multi-Sectoral Technical and Economic Cooperation (BIMSTEC). A conglomerate of seven countries (Bangladesh, Bhutan, Myanmar, India, Nepal, Sri Lanka and Thailand) from South and Southeast Asia, it is home to one-fifth of the world's population with rich energy and mineral reserves. For India, the forum is visualised as a framework that could connect and develop India's long-neglected northeast[38] – also enumerated in the 2014 BJP manifesto – as a priority agenda for the government. Scholars have argued that the economic integration of northeast India will "liberate" the region from its geographical handicap of being "landlocked and lead to significant strategic dividends".[39]

Apart from pushing an early conclusion of the BIMSTEC FTA,[40] the Indian government has been aiming to improve physical connectivity through various projects such as the India-Myanmar-Thailand Trilateral Highway,[41] the Kaladan Multimodal Transit Transport Project,[42] the Asian Highway Network, the ASEAN Master Plan for Connectivity, a sea-link via the Sittwe port in Myanmar and several others. Enhancing connectivity through these initiatives has been the catchword given their criticality for India's economic development (particularly of the northeast) and meeting security concerns. However, projects like the Kaladan are also facing problems given that a 109-km road from Zorinpui (Mizoram) to Paletwa (Mynmar) is still missing and without a road link the entire project stands sunk.[43] Similarly, the Trilateral Highways has also not been able to achieve success and has been criticised by the ASEAN countries for its slow progress during the International Media Conference 2016.[44] The next section will discuss India's connectivity initiatives in more detail.

Another cross-regional initiative that India has been engaged in is the Mekong-Ganga Cooperation (MGC). Launched in 2000 in Lao PDR, it involves five Southeast Asian countries namely Cambodia, Lao PDR, Myanmar, Thailand and Vietnam, apart from India, for increasing cooperation in sectors like tourism, education and culture. The initiative demonstrates India's focus on the CLMV Group of countries in the region. Transport and communication for increasing connectivity between the CLMV and India is also being emphasised for deepening economic exchange and strategic partnership.[45] New areas like health research, sharing of expertise on epidemic management, food security and preserving the rich biodiversity of the region, while bringing together the complementarities that exist in the Small and Medium Enterprises (SME) sector in India and the CLMV countries, are also being focused upon.

India's efforts at regionalism were results of both economic and geostrategic imperatives. Its external economic policies adopted from the 1990s gelled well with the LEP resulting in greater engagement with Southeast Asia and Asia-Pacific through economic tools. But a deeper engagement with the region was also inspired by realpolitik and power ambitions. The closer association with the ASEAN and participation in the ASEAN-centric regional architecture has helped India in gaining a footprint in the strategic order of the region. The league has also been instrumental in projecting a confident India capable of reaping more long-term strategic benefits of its association with the ASEAN and regional forums by adding strategic aspects to economic engagement. This is manifesting through efforts at building regional connectivity, particularly with the geographically contiguous countries of Southeast Asia and in intensifying maritime cooperation with partners in Southeast Asia and beyond. These efforts impart a new dimension to the evolving regional order given the prominence of connectivity-based projects like China's OBOR influencing regional security. However, India's slow progress on projects like the Kaladan, to an extent, damage India's image raising questions about India's implementation and execution policies.

ECONOMIC ENGAGEMENT

Many Southeast Asian countries look at India as a possible locomotive for regional growth while considering it an important counterbalance to China's dominating presence in the region. India, on its part, has also been equally eager to deepen its economic relations while playing a major power role in Southeast Asia.[46] With China's territorial claims disturbing the region and the new US President Donald Trump's strategy on Asia yet to assume clarity, it is perhaps the right time for India to pursue a long-term comprehensive strategy towards the region.

As we observed in the last section, India has been strengthening its economic ties with the ASEAN Member States (AMS) through the various ASEAN-centric forums. However, economic engagement still has considerable potential for improvement, given that India is yet to become as large a trade partner or as important a destination/source for investment as Southeast Asia's Eastern neighbours like Japan, Korea and China are for it. With the US pulling out of the TPP[47] – the largest mega-regional trade agreement which could bind Singapore, Malaysia, Brunei and Vietnam to large economies like US and Canada on the Pacific Rim – the region is struggling to cope with the disappointment. The problems with the TPP are likely to hasten negotiations on the RCEP,[48] thus providing India with an opportunity to play a bigger role within the mega-trade agreement and consequently in the economic architecture of the Asia-Pacific. A successful RCEP could create the momentum for the establishment of an FTA of the Asia-Pacific, facilitating greater economic activities between India and the region.[49] India's willingness to compromise on its earlier restrictive tariff offers[50] indicates that New Delhi is viewing the RCEP as a platform for significantly increasing its share of trade and investment with the region. As argued further by Palit, since the RCEP is not a collection of China's defence allies unlike the TPP, which is a collective of the US defence allies, the grouping is less likely to be dominated by China with all the RCEP member countries getting the opportunity to shape the structure and framework of the agreement.[51]

There is little doubt that the RCEP could provide India the opportunity for greater economic engagement with the region at a time when its trade ties with Southeast Asia are improving steadily. India's trade with Southeast Asia has expanded more than ten-fold from US$7.1 billion to US$74.4 billion during 2000-01 to 2013-14. However, as pointed out earlier, India's economic interactions with the entire region is not only below potential but is also not uniform. The cross-border capital flows have been particularly high with Singapore and much less with the other Southeast Asian countries. The island country is not only becoming a major source of FDI into India, but is a principal destination for outward FDI flows as well. With the coming into force of the India-ASEAN services and investment agreement in 2015, there is an expectation of easier movement of professionals from India to the region and more investments. However, India has a very long way to go before it can match the economic presences of China and Japan in the region. The role of connectivity is particularly important in enhancing India's economic linkages with the region. Working with Southeast Asian countries for facilitating transport transit and border trade for a greater integration of the Indian industries in regional value chains[52] is a priority for India and is consistent with the AEP's long-term economic goals, especially for deepening economic partnerships with the AMS.[53]

While several enterprises are underway between India and the ASEAN for strengthening economic linkages, India has been engaging the region through several economic initiatives including infrastructure-building, development assistance[54] and investments. India's strategy of actively participating in infrastructure-building in the region and providing development assistance and investment is guided by multiple motivations. The first is related to its own economic development. As India has been emerging a major power with immense economic prospects, its leadership has been aggressive on expanding economic links with neighbours and regions. A rapid growth of the Indian economy would increase the demand for markets and access to resources in a manner similar to the impact of China's rapid growth. It is in keeping with these demands that the Indian leadership has been increasingly focusing on developing infrastructure thereby enhancing connectivity within the region[55] while offering development assistance and investments.

The second objective has a greater connection with India's image-building in the region. Assisting infrastructure-building in relatively economically backward countries like Cambodia, Laos and Myanmar that produce considerable benefits for the locals by expanding the stock of public goods and services contributes significantly to India's image in the region. The effort fits well with the ASEAN's goal of focusing on the newer members for facilitating their economic development and bridging the economic gap between the CLMV countries and the rest of the ASEAN. Increasing connectivity, apart from providing market and accessing natural resources, also helps to expand people-to-people communication. Initiatives such as the ASEAN Framework Agreement on the Facilitation of Cross Border Transport Passenger by Road Vehicles (ASEAN CBTP) are specifically geared to support greater intra-ASEAN social and cultural interaction amongst its people.[56] Finally, given China's rapidly growing economic presence and strategic foothold in South Asia, India is eager to project itself as a country which is willing to engage beyond its immediate neighbourhood and more importantly, in China's backyard.

Development assistance has emerged an important foreign policy tool with a Development Administration Partnership (DPA)[57] being created in the MEA in January 2012 to effectively handle India's aid projects through various stages such as concept, launch, execution and completion for example.[58] New Delhi offers development partnership based on the needs identified by partner countries with the MEA trying to accommodate as many requests as possible, given their technical and financial feasibilities.[59] Such assistance has been offered to Myanmar, which has emerged a major recipient of Indian grants and loans out of the total development assistance committed between 2000-01 and 2013-14.[60] This also indicates the significance of Myanmar in India's foreign policy. Several Lines of Credit (LOCs) have been made to the other countries as well including Laos, Cambodia and Vietnam while offering soft loans to Indonesia for developing the power infrastructure.[61] Cambodia is also receiving grants-in-aid and financial assistance from India for setting up the MGC Asian Traditional Textiles Museum at Siem Reap under the MGC scheme.

Going beyond development assistance, India's investment strategy in Southeast Asia highlights New Delhi's long-term need for resources and raw materials. India has been investing heavily in Vietnam (in sectors such as energy, mineral exploration, agro-processing), Myanmar (telecommunication, energy, aviation), Indonesia (oil and gas, coal mining), Cambodia (agro processing, mining, oil and gas) and Laos (iron ore mining, agro-wood). Such investments are complementary to the plans for expanding connectivity. Developing infrastructure for enhancing cross-border connectivity has been a major priority for all the AMS countries and India's proactive role on connectivity has increased India's importance to the region. However, such connectivity plans also entail added pressure for better integration. For example, with the AEC established in 2015 aiming for a large and more integrated market, there is a pressure on India to better understand regional business systems, economic practices and institutions for integrating better.

The enhancement of intraregional transport infrastructure is another area of converging interest, though, it is of course not a new priority for India and its neighbours. With an eye to improving logistics for reducing transport time and costs, apart from the overall enhancement of intraregional transport infrastructure, the BIMSTEC Transport Infrastructure and Logistics Study (BTILS) examined the prospects for developing infrastructure for enhancing connectivity between India and the AMS in 2008. The Delhi Dialogue alluded to earlier, has also discussed augmenting connectivity within the region (most importantly land and sea). Connectivity also figured prominently on the agenda of the ASEAN Summit in New Delhi in 2012, when the Indian Prime Minister Manmohan Singh mentioned: "Connectivity – physical, institutional, people-to-people, digital, and by sea and air – holds the key to closer partnership between India and ASEAN".[62] Subsequently, after two years, a similar sentiment was again reflected by the Indian PM Modi when he visited Myanmar for attending the ASEAN summit in 2014.[63] The Summit in 2012, apart from calling for completion of the India-Myanmar-Thailand Trilateral Highway and extending it to Laos and Cambodia, also called for finalisation of the Kaladan Multimodal Transit Transport Project (KMTTP) connecting Kolkata with Sittwe in Myanmar by sea. The Indian and regional leaderships also urged completion of a new highway project connecting India-Myanmar-Lao-Vietnam-Cambodia and developing the Mekong-India Economic Corridor (MIEC) for integrating the four Mekong countries – Myanmar, Thailand, Cambodia and Vietnam – with India.

Economic infrastructure-building and connectivity projects are not limited to land and highways alone and are extending to maritime connectivity as well. Major port projects are being planned to link India's eastern and northeastern states to Myanmar, Thailand and beyond. A multimodal transport project mentioned earlier, connecting India's landlocked northeast and its eastern seaport of Kolkata with Myanmar via sea, a waterway and road, has also been progressing, though behind schedule.[64] New Delhi is also working on a 3,200-kilometre highway that would run through the northeastern states, Myanmar and the northern Thai provinces (Chiang Mai and Chiang Rai), where it could link with roads to Laos, Cambodia and Vietnam. The construction of railways, identified as another ASEAN-India integrator for expanding connectivity, has also been underway in India's northeast (Assam and Manipur) to connect to Myanmar. Further, the Indian Railways' decision to be a part of the Trans-Asian Railway Link between Europe and Southeast Asia via Iran, Pakistan, India, Bangladesh, Myanmar, Thailand and Malaysia – is being considered by the United Nations Economics and Social Commission for Asia and the Pacific (UNESCAP) under the Asian Land Infrastructure Development Project that emphasises India's commitment to pan-regional connectivity and infrastructure development. Given that communicating positive images constitute a considerable part of national image-building, projecting India as a major stakeholder in regional connectivity and infrastructure initiatives does help in enhancing its acceptability across regional constituencies.

Finally, economic engagement and image-building can hardly overlook tourism, which, apart from earning foreign exchange for the country, contributes to India's global and regional "appeal". Tourist inflows between India and Southeast Asia have been increasing over time. Tourism has emerged a priority between India and Malaysia for facilitating people-to-people movement between the two countries. But obviously there is a considerable scope for further improvement. Efforts to increase tourism by projecting India's culture and heritage to receptive audiences in the region can work well. northeast India is particularly significant in this respect. The region still does not figure as a coveted destination for international tourists. India is keen on showcasing the northeast as a tourist destination by improving its infrastructure and it is here that New Delhi's connectivity projects with neighbouring countries become critical. Introduction of e-visas along with a wide range of marketing tools like "Incredible India" are also important for increasing tourist flows from Southeast Asia.[65] But more can be done in terms of expanding the scope of effective initiatives, particularly if they are compared with large-scale efforts by a country like Indonesia that now offers free visa-on-arrival to more than 150 countries.

Tourism and people-to-people communication can also increase from greater cooperation in aviation. India's aviation cooperation with countries in Southeast Asia remains disappointing compared to the US and many European countries. While there are no direct flights connecting Delhi to Jakarta – the headquarters of the ASEAN or Manila[66] – the headquaters of the Asian Development Bank (ADB) – the air connnections with the CLMV countries are even worse with no direct flight connecting New Delhi to any of the CLMV country capitals. Of course, Singapore, Malaysia and Thailand are densely integrated with Indian cities through multiple air links. But their greater integration, compared with scant connections of the rest of Southeast Asia, only reinforces the lack of uniformity that is conspicuous in India's economic engagement with the region.

CULTURAL ENGAGEMENT

While power play on the one hand and increased cooperation on the other dominate India's interface with the region in the 21st century, cultural engagement is increasingly becoming important. Similar to India, cultural diversity and plurality are the defining characteristics of Southeast Asia as well. With most countries of the region endowed with diverse culture, history and heritage – a lot of which is shared as briefly discussed in the last chapter – intercultural communication and engagement between the states in the region is only logical. Pronounced cultural interaction is also the hallmark of enhanced people-to-people communication, as rightly pointed out by Villanueva Rivas, given that "a lasting and stable world order cannot rely merely on governments and power politics; it also depends on the free exchange of cultures among peoples in pursuing common intellectual and cultural interests via open cosmopolitan public and cultural diplomacies".[67] While facilitating greater interaction amongst people is a coveted objective for the larger good, culture is also a tool for allaying mutual misconceptions and promoting harmony and understanding, while at the same time contributing to national "images" of big powers.

The role of cultural diplomacy (CD) in modern international engagement can hardly be overstated. The relevance of cultural initiatives to the ASEAN countries has been aptly surmised by Tan See Seng: "For a regional community that is substantive, you can't do without that socio-cultural. What that essentially means is getting the level of civil society across the board, across ASEAN countries to co-hear, to come together, to be engaging one another as it were...".[68] On the other hand, Harvey B. Feigenbaum points out that the primary aim of modern cultural policies of nations is creating economic value through the accumulation of cultural capital. He argues that the "new economy is a knowledge-based, and knowledge is acquired through institutions that are shaped by culture...therefore, cultural wealth of nations is the key to the New Economy".[69] Thus, cultural wealth has become critical in the discourse on CD while highlighting the role culture plays in economics. These functions of culture have motivated the AMS to make cultural communication an important element of the regional cooperation agenda. Notwithstanding the emphasis, cultural communication largely remains low key in Southeast Asia when compared to intra-regional economic interactions. This "cautious" cultural interaction is perhaps a deliberate Indian policy since India does not want to be seen as a neighbour aggressively imposing its culture on the region. Also India's historical cultural interaction with the region was "borrowed" as was earlier mentioned in the chapter, thus highlighting ancient India's "peaceful" cultural interaction with its neighbours. The attempt is therefore to aim at mutual intercultural communication which will further help India's image as a country celebrating distinct cultures instead.

The ASEAN Declaration of 1967 – the year the grouping was formed in Bangkok – outlined the promotion of active collaboration and mutual assistance on matters of common cultural interest in addition to those in economic, social, technical, scientific and administrative fields as important goals to be achieved.[70] The

Declaration also put down cooperation in educational, professional, technical and administrative spheres for bolstering bilateral ties. In addition to the directions and emphasis provided in the Declaration, the ASEAN Socio-Cultural Community (ASCC)[71] aims to increase communication between the people of the region and has several people-oriented initiatives. Adopted on the occasion of the 19th ASEAN Summit in Bali in November 2011, the Declaration on ASEAN Unity in Cultural Diversity seeks to instil a sense of belonging and to enhance deeper mutual understanding about cultures, religions and civilisations. With a plan to engage the youth of the region – the future of a nation after all lies in the hands of its posterity – a series of activities under the theme "Festival of ASEAN Cultural Expressions", together with several other cultural and art initiatives are being implemented. The ongoing initiatives include efforts to involve the social media and networks to realise the Declaration and assist in connecting peoples and bridging cultures for attaining One ASEAN Community.[72] In addition, bilateral cultural communication is also gradually being pushed by the governments as part of the overall bilateral relationship.

In the context of viewing India's cultural engagement and diplomatic initiatives with Southeast Asia, it is important to note that the histories of India and Southeast Asia have influenced the former's cultural communication with the region. As already pointed out earlier, the "Indianisation" of Southeast Asia through the ancient times marked by selective "localisation" of Indian cultural elements, was never "imposed" but "borrowed" by the Southeast Asian rulers for legitimacy. This aspect has earned India phenomenal plaudits which in turn imparts it with a strategic edge in "image" as compared with China, enabling it to pursue soft power more seamlessly with the region. This is important given that elsewhere in its immediate neighbourhood of South Asia, India is occasionally perceived as overtly entrenching itself. India could be conscious of avoiding such impressions in Southeast Asia, particularly that of a "cultural coloniser".

Perhaps, flowing out of India's hesitation to aggressively "export" culture, Indian cinema, a pronounced non-state actor, is conspicuous in New Delhi's foreign policymaking and CD. Defined by Joseph

Montville as an "unofficial diplomacy" (or "Track Two diplomacy") in which non-state actors seek to improve international communication, Indian cinema has been contributing extensively to India's soft power in Southeast Asian countries and beyond. Movies have been great ambassadors of India and its culture in Indonesia, Myanmar, Thailand, Laos, Brunei and in the rest of the region where Indian High Commissions and Consulates regularly screens movies. The Centenary celebration of Indian Cinema in Jakarta in 2013 was seen as an important platform for enhancing people-to-people communication and cross-cultural linkages. Indonesian filmmakers have also brought their cinema to the Indian audience, thus trying to achieve what is an ideal scenario of cross-cultural sharing and exchanges, underlying the principle of "listening to others", as well as "showing a desire to learn from them". Movie screenings have also been able to cut across a variety of audiences as is evident from the regular holding of Indian film festivals in major regional university campuses like the National University of Singapore (NUS). Movies bolster other institutional efforts like cultural exchanges as well. India also has several government-initiated Cultural Exchange Programmes (CEPs) with Malaysia, Philippines, Indonesia, Laos, Myanmar, Singapore and Vietnam. In addition to Southeast Asia, there is the Australian Cultural Visits Programme seeking to strengthen people-to-people exchanges and cultural linkages between India and Australia.

India-Japan cultural relations have a long history, similar to that of Southeast Asia and India. Since 1978, Japan has been extending cultural grant aid to Indian research institutes, universities and cultural faculty for encouraging research and other related activities. In addition, through the UNESCO/Japan Trust Fund for Preservation of the World Cultural Heritage, Japan is assisting India with the preservation and restoration of the Buddhist monuments of Sanchi and Satdhara.[73] This is an example of Buddhism and religion being a conduit for strengthening Indian-Japanese ties and international partnerships.[74] The Japan Foundation, which opened its office in New Delhi way back in 1994, apart from focusing on teaching Japanese, has also been actively engaged in promoting bilateral cultural relations.

Education, within the purview of culture, has also been identified as an area for collaboration by the ASEAN leaders. The ASCC, apart from pushing cooperation amongst the ASEAN countries through culture, also recognises the role of education while proposing 28 action lines relevant to education for implementation by 2015.[75] While the ASEAN 5-Year Work Plan on Education (2011-2015) was incorporated in 2011, the Plan also listed four priorities and 20 specific programmes for implementation again by 2015. Education can definitely provide interesting opportunities for expanding bilateral and regional cooperation between India and Southeast Asia.

Till now, India's education cooperation with the region has been low as compared with China. China's growth as a regional education hub poses challenges for India in pitching itself as an alternative location with scope and variety in deepening long-term education cooperation. *The Economic Survey* (2010-11) stressed the need to develop India as an education hub, while the erstwhile Planning Commission of India argued that the widespread use of English and cheaper living costs can help India in becoming a global hub for higher education. The "internationalisation" of education has found favour with the Narendra Modi government with a UPA-era proposal that was once opposed by the BJP, being now revived by the Niti Aayog[76] in its report submitted in 2015. The proposal supports inviting foreign universities to open campuses in the country to meet the demand for higher education in India, and to increase competition among service providers and improve overall standards of higher education in the country.[77] However, to what extent this proposal is geared for attracting foreign students to Indian universities is not too clear at this point.

With cross-border higher education increasingly becoming important in hastening global integration, India has been eager to explore enabling possibilities given that it is the third largest higher education system in the world next to the USA and China. India has been offering scholarships to Southeast Asian countries like Malaysia under various schemes like the AYUSH scholarship scheme, General Cultural Scholarship Scheme, Education Exchange Programme (EEP) and the Indian Scholarship and Trust Fund. India has been providing scholarships to Lao nationals through the Indian Technical and Economic Cooperation (ITEC), the TCS Colombo Plan, the Mekong-

Ganga Cooperation Scholarship Scheme and the General Cultural Scholarship Scheme.[78] The Philippines is also one of the beneficiaries of the ITEC and the Colombo Plan. To encourage Indonesian students to look at India as an option for higher education, a special publication titled "Studying in India" in the Bahasa language was also brought out, as part of the commemorative events marking twenty years of the India-ASEAN partnership in 2012.

The ASEAN has also provided a forum for greater interaction between India and its Southeast Asian neighbours in education. This includes establishing English-language training facilities like the Lao India Centre for English Language, which was set up in Vientiane on June 12, 2007. The ASEAN-India Students Exchange Programme has been popular between India and the Philippines while similar Student Exchange Programmes have been employed by India to connect to countries like Thailand as well. A model programme for educational and professional exchange – India Research Initiatives by the NUS – has emerged to facilitate greater collaborations between the University and leading Indian universities and institutes through short-term visits of academic staff, long-term research collaborations, visit of graduate students, and summer intern programmes for Indian undergraduate and graduate students interested in working at the NUS. The Indian Council for Cultural Relations (ICCR) has established a Tagore Chair of Contemporary Indian Studies in Ho Chih Minh (Vietnam) to help propagate studies related to India while there are other ICCR Chairs in Singapore, including Hindi and Sanskrit Chairs in Thailand, Sanskrit and Buddhist Studies in Cambodia and many short-term Chairs in Singapore, Thailand, Indonesia, Japan and Australia.[79] India and Australia are also eager to bolster education cooperation with the Indian and Australian Education Ministers meeting regularly for Ministerial Dialogues on Education Cooperation and more and more Indian students opting to go to Australia for pursuing further studies.

High-Level Bilateral Visits

Both Realists and Constructivists recognise the role of communication and dialogue – an ongoing, continuous process with its own logic and rhythm – as being critical in diplomacy.[80] While the former consider good diplomacy as essential in interstate competition, the latter attach importance to signals, symbols and persuasive tools of diplomacy that shape norms and beliefs about interest, and can influence behaviour as well. High-level visits conform to both schools of thought with their emphasis on dialogue, symbolism and communication while conducting "good" diplomacy. These visits, which are independent tools of statecraft, facilitate effective diplomacy. Foreign visits by senior leaders involving dramatic fanfare often go down as important turning points in crafting diplomatic relationships. While leaders occasionally deliver historic speeches and communicate nuanced messages on foreign soil, face-to-face diplomacy through visits, according to Morgenthau, allow leaders to maintain or open channels that provide critical information and facilitate vital communication among governments in the pursuit of their interests.[81] Face-to-face diplomacy also helps in assessing other states' intentions and agendas.[82]

High-level visits by Indian leaders from time to time are in keeping with the larger national objectives of achieving economic development and for cooperating with neighbours while reinforcing India's intent to project itself as an important player at the regional level. The LEP is an appropriate example. It is hardly surprising that the LEP was first officially defined and articulated by the then Indian Prime Minister Rao during his visit to Singapore in 1994. During his visit, Rao had not only stressed India's ancient historical and cultural relations with the region with "India looking towards reinforcing cooperative linkages with its eastern neighbours", but also emphasised "on building strong economic and security relationship between India and its Eastern neighbours",[83] thus communicating the government's firm resolve to engage with the region. The visits were maintained by the next Prime Minister, Atal Bihari Vajpayee, who made the most visits to Southeast Asia – four in about two years – by travelling to seven of the ten Southeast Asian countries (except Brunei, the Philippines and Myanmar). There were reciprocal visits from the leaders of Malaysia, Singapore and Indonesia as well, all of whom stressed on shared Asian values during their visits for setting the stage for economic relations to take off from the ground and flourish. Prime Minister Manmohan Singh chose Thailand for his maiden visit while Prime Minister Modi visited Myanmar within the first few months of assuming office unveiling the AEP there. Prime Minister Modi's decision to attend the funeral of the late Lee Kuan Yew in 2015, the first Prime Minister and founding father of Singapore, was largely symbolic and conveyed India's solidarity and support to Singapore.

High-level visits while conveying strategic intentions can be used to communicate "hard" messages as well. Vietnam's decision to renew India's lease of two oil blocks in the South China Sea, which irked China, came on the eve of India's External Affairs Minister Sushma Swaraj's visit to Vietnam in August 2014. Both sides employed the visit to communicate multiple messages to China: one, that India has a major commercial stake in the region where territorial disputes between Southeast Asian nations and China have threatened regional peace and two, Vietnam is keen to have India as a long-term ally, playing the role of a regional balancer. The Minister's visit, her first foreign visit, underlined the significance India attached to Vietnam and was also meant to communicate to the region India's decision and determination to pursue a robust foreign policy that reflected a growing self-confidence. The External Affairs Minister's visit was followed by the President of India, Pranab Mukherjee's visit to Vietnam the following month, coinciding with President Xi Jinping's visit to India, and sent off interesting geostrategic connotations. In a similar vein, the Indian Vice President Hamid Ansari's visits to Brunei and Indonesia in late 2015 signalled the strategic value of both countries to India in its efforts to move forward on a regional order that involves a more proactive India and was also probably meant to signal India's committment to containing religious radicalisation, a concern looming large in Brunei and Idnonesia. Prime Minister Modi's visit to Australia, Japan, Singapore and Malaysia were also undertaken to achieve multiple objectives, including mobilising investments, engaging the large Indian diaspora and for sourcing nuclear supplies.

* * *

India, often perceived a "reactive" force, has been looking for strategic space both at the regional as well as at the global level. Its image-building efforts are closely linked to its determination to play a bigger role at the regional and the global systemic. New Delhi is aware that as a power it is yet to "arrive". But its ambition of playing a more proactive role and having a greater say in regional and global affairs has been steadily imparting a distinct activism in India's foreign policy, which, as a result, is undergoing a significant transformation with pragmatism increasingly displacing ideology.

While a tendency to play a big power role is clearly visible with New Delhi designing ways and means for enhanced engagement through various policies discussed in the chapter, there is little doubt that India's economic growth and bright future economic prospects are instrumental behind the activism noted in foreign policy. Domestic issues, however, occasionally pose constraints, particularly India's hesitant and somewhat defensive external trade policies, which are roadblocks to deepening India's economic engagement with Southeast Asia and the Asia-Pacific. Coupled with domestic constraints, India's delay in enforcing policies and executing projects, especially connectivity initiatives, are in sharp contrast to China which is known for its strong state machinery and quick delivering capacity. Successive Indian leaderships have been working towards developing an effective strategy that combines its aspirations and interests – economic, strategic and geopolitical – but a lot of ground still needs to be covered. Indeed, CD too is largely dependent on economic engagement given that such engagement creates more opportunities for cultural communication. However, the lack of capacity in India's foreign policy establishment could be a factor styming its activism in the neighbourhood. As pointed out by some scholars, India's "foreign policy capacity remains the smallest not only among the G-20 countries but also in the BRICS group of countries to take on the responsibility that is being asked of it."[84] Unless that is addressed both quantitatively and qualitatively, the government's bold initiatives might come to naught.

The formulation of the LEP in the early 1990s and the AEP subsequently vindicates India's focus and attention on sealing cooperative collaborations with the extended neighbourhood beyond stratified frontiers. While the LEP tried to set the stage for enhanced economic, security and cultural collaboration with its neighbours through greater participation in ASEAN-centric forums and the regional architecture, the AEP aims to further consolidate and deepen existing relationships and take the collaboration to far-flung corners of the Asia-Pacific beyond Southeast Asia. As an upgraded edition of the LEP, the AEP has not shied away from conveying India's intentions of becoming a more active player in the regional strategic dynamics, including the aspiration to be a provider of security. This is evident from the decision to sell the Akash missile system to Vietnam and a maritime cooperation with Australia and Indonesia for securing the Indo-Pacific SLOCs. India's ambitions have been sought to be conveyed to the region through the projection of a confident, responsible and proactive India, particularly through high-level visits that have carried nuanced messages and signals for the regional audiences and core constituencies. The projection has made successive Indian leaderships sensitive about the importance of an image make-over given the growth in India's long-term power ambitions. The challenge is to maintain the projection in a manner that keeps the Indian image in the region virtuous while enabling India to progress on its long-term ambitions.

ENDNOTES

1. 'Indian Foreign Policy: A Road Map for the Decade Ahead'
2. India's "neighbourhood" also comprises Central Asia, West Asia and the Indian Ocean along with Southeast Asia.
3. Pant, 'India has to do more to fix its Southeast Asian relations'
4. India decided to "break out of the claustrophobic confines of South Asia" towards the end of the 1990s. See Scott
5. Chanda, 'S-E Asia still important to India's development and security'
6. Schweller, 'Managing the rise of Great Powers: History and Theory': 1-31
7. Rao, *India and the Asia-Pacific: Forging a New Relationship*: 2
8. Many scholars believe that the LEP was first initiated in 1991 and later in 1993 Rao delineated it in South Korea calling for economic liberalisation and an "opening in the floodgates" to South Korean chaebols (mega corporations). For details see Reischer, 'India's Look East policy in the South China Sea'
9. According to Arvind Gupta, "In keeping with its bid for a leadership role in Asia and beyond, India seeks greater integration with ASEAN and is striving to create an Asian Economic Community. Looking back, it can be said that the Policy has been moderately successful". For details see Gupta, 'Myanmar's critical role in bolstering India's Look East Policy'
10. According to Paul Evans, regionalism is "the expression of a common sense of identity and destiny combined with the creation of institutions that express that identity and shape collective action."

11. Rosecrance, 'Regionalism and the Post-Cold War Era': 373–393.
12. Washington mostly remained inattentive towards the region prior to 2001. With the 9/11, President Bush labeled Southeast Asia as 'second front' of terrorism thus refocusing on the region once again.
13. India's idea of regionalism was partly fashioned out of its geographical proximity to the Southeast Asian region (apart from South Asia) and other specificities (Edward Mansfield and Helen Milner 1997) conditioning its foreign policy towards the region. See Mansfield, Milner
14. India's domestic compulsions (financial crises, increasing terrorism and insurgency) as well as regional developments (the emergence of Sagiang Division of Myanmar as a safe haven for the insurgent groups of northeast India, Pakistan adopting a more determined anti-India stance, reflecting in the encouragement and aiding of militants in J&K and its attempt to internationalise developments in J&K since the 1990s) required India to look beyond South Asia and connect to its neighbours to its East.
15. ASEAN-India dialogue relations have provided India with opportunities to participate in consultative meetings which include Summits, ministerial meetings and similar other forums for enhancing regional dialogue and accelerating regional integration while ensuring political and security cooperation, economic cooperation and socio-cultural cooperation amongst them.
16. Chatterjee, 'The Look East Policy and India's northeastern States'
17. Both Australia (first dialogue partner of ASEAN in 1974) and Japan (became dialogue partner in 1977) have been dialogue partners with the ASEAN since the 1970s.
18. It was not until the end of March 1994 that the balance of payments crisis was clearly over with foreign exchange reserves rising. Export growth rate was also seen improving.
19. Ray, 'India's Act East Policy: A track record and recommendations for the future'
20. Palit, 'India-Southeast Asia relations: enhancing mutual benefits'
21. Pillalamarri, 'Why India should 'Look West' instead'
22. The former Indian Prime Minister Manmohan Singh had made a case for "an Asian Economic Community combining Japan, Asean countries, China, India and South Korea as an 'arc of advantage' across which there will be large-scale movement of people, capital, ideas and creativity." For details see Lintner, 'India-ASEAN Economic Relations'
23. While the expert working groups, established in 2011, have been focusing on "soft" areas like humanitarian assistance and disaster relief, military medicine, counter terrorism , peace-keeping and maritime security, their objective may not be completely 'soft'.
24. 'ASEAN Defense Ministers Meeting Plus'
25. The China Pakistan Economic Corridor (CPEC) will help Beijing to expand its maritime capabilities particularly in the IOR.
26. Baruah, 'Japan: India's unique maritime partner'
27. Koh, 'Toward a Japan-Singapore-India maritime partnership'
28. Mohan, *Modi's World*: 146

29. Kugelman, 'India acts East'
30. 'Here's how Modi has strengthened India's Navy'
31. The Delhi Dialogue began in 2009 and there have been eight editions till 2017.
32. Parashar, 'India to invite heads of 10 Asean nations for Republic Day celebrations'
33. Chaulia, *Modi Doctrine*
34. Palit, Sinha, *Analysing China's Soft Power Strategy and Comparable Indian Initiatives*
35. Das, 'India-ASEAN Defense Relations'
36. Ibid
37. Sajjanhar, 'Taking stock of India's "Act Easy Policy"'
38. India's northeast comprise of Assam, Meghalaya, Manipur, Mizoram, Tripura, Nagaland and Arunachal Pradesh, popularly referred to as the seven sisters. Sikkim is also constitutionally and technically a part of this category but its location and history makes it unique among the northeastern states.
39. Das, 'India's Look East Policy: Imagining a New Geography of India's Northeast': 348-349
40. The Indian government not only sought an early conclusion of the proposed BIMSTEC FTA at the meeting in 2016 but also softened its stance on the trade agreement.
41. Started in 2005, it is a more important project that promises to establish road connectivity from the Manipur border to Thailand through Myanmar. But little progress has been achieved on this project. For details see Bose, 'All's not quiet on the eastern front'
42. The Kaladan project, started in 2008, is a road-river-port cargo transport collaboration between India and Myanmar to ensure alternate connectivity to Mizoram. Apart from boosting the economy of Myanmar, the project will pose as an alternative route for goods from India's northeast to rest of the country and the world.
43. Bose, 'All's not quiet on the eastern front'
44. Ibid
45. New areas of cooperation between India and the region were identified in September 2012 when India hosted the Sixth MGC Ministerial Meeting in New Delhi.
46. During the India-Philippines third joint commission meeting on bilateral affairs in October 2015 in New Delhi, India decided to support Manila in its dispute over the islands in the South China Sea (the Philippines calls the South China Sea the West Philippine Sea after the escalation of its maritime dispute with China) with Beijing, underlying India's choice for activism in the region.
47. The Trans-Pacific Partnership (TPP) is a comprehensive trade and investment agreement aiming to reduce barriers and tariffs among the United States and 11 other Pacific Rim nations. A hallmark of the Obama administration, President Trump, on assuming office, decided to withdraw from it in January 2017 by signing an Executive Order.
48. The RCEP is a 16-member bloc comprising of 10 ASEAN members and their six free trade agreement partners – India, China, Japan, Korea, Australia and New Zealand. With more than one-third of the global economy and almost half of the

world's population, the RCEP is a powerful economic grouping, large enough to create one of the world's biggest free trade areas offering significant new economic opportunities for its members.

49. Palit, 'RCEP has to be more inclusive than TPP'
50. Palit, 'India inches towards liberalisation at RCEP'
51. There are many members in the RCEP, for instance Vietnam, with whom China has difficult political relations.
52. Palit, 'India-Southeast Asia Relations: Enhancing mutual benefits'
53. The Indian budget (2015-16) includes a proposal to set up Special Purpose Vehicle for facilitating India's investment in CLMV countries.
54. Development Assistance can be in the form of soft loans, aid, grants, and non-financial assistance like technical assistance.
55. India's role in infrastructure development, especially with Myanmar, is also planned for connecting India's underdeveloped northeast to Southeast Asia.
56. 'The Twentieth ASEAN Transport Ministers Meeting'
57. Development Partnerships comprises of training (through ITEC), Lines of Credit (EXIM Bank) and grants (handled by the DPA).
58. 'Development Partnership Administration'
59. Ibid
60. Mullen, 'India's Development Assistance: Will it change the global development finance paradigm?'
61. 'Overview: ASEAN-India Dialogue Relations'
62. Osius, 'Enhancing India-ASEAN Connectivity'
63. In his address at the ASEAN summit in Myanmar in November 2014, PM Modi stated: "to deepen our connectivity, I am considering establishing, with your cooperation, a special facility or special purpose vehicle to facilitate project financing and quick implementation"
64. 'India's new gateway to ASEAN'
65. 'India expects 9 lakh South East Asian tourists this year'
66. However, there are many direct flights to Singapore from many Indian cities daily.
67. Rivas, 'Cosmopolitan Constructivism'
68. 'ASEAN Community at the top of the agenda for 2015 summit'
69. Kang, 'Reframing Cultural Diplomacy: International Cultural Politics of Soft Power and the Creative Economy'
70. 'The ASEAN Declaration (Bangkok Declaration) Bangkok'
71. One of the pillars of an ambitious plan of creating an ASEAN Community is the ASCC. The other two pillars are the ASEAN Economic Community and Political-Security Community.
72. 'ASEAN Socio-Cultural Community (ASCC)'
73. 'The History of Japanese-Indian Exchange'
74. The Nalanda University, which began its first academic session on September 1, 2014 with 15 students, is another multi-nation project that has seen many Southeast Asian countries, including China, joining hands with India.
75. 'ASEAN State of Education Report 2013'

76. Niti Ayog is a Government of India think-tank established by the Narendra Modi government replacing the Planning Commission.
77. Chopra, 'Allow foreign university campuses, says Niti Ayog'
78. 'Brief on India-Laos Bilateral Relations'
79. 'List of ICCR operational Hindi Chairs'
80. Lebovic, Saunders, 'The Diplomatic Core: How the United States employs high-level visits as a scarce resource'
81. Ibid
82. Hall, Yarhi-Milo, 'The Personal Touch: Leaders' impressions, costly signalling and assessments of sincerity in international affairs'
83. Muni, 'India's 'Look East Policy': the strategic dimension'
84. Sidhu, Godbole, 'Modi's foreign policy@365: course action'

4

China and Southeast Asia: New Paradigms for Cooperation in the Modern World

China's foreign policy during the recent years reflects both power and reassurance – "a balancing act designed to secure a positive interactive process between its rise and world politics"[1] – and is driven by the objective of cultivating positive foreign reactions and projecting strength. The Chinese leadership is apprised of the need to "build a sound and stable framework of major-country relations" and "strengthen unity and cooperation with other developing countries"[2] which, to a great extent, determine China's contemporary foreign interactions with neighbours and the world and shape its approach towards region-building and multilateralism while projecting "assertiveness". China's emphasis on "strength" was articulated by the CCP's Central Committee in 2009 when it underlined "four strengths" that should dictate China's foreign policy: attaining greater influence in international politics, strengthening competitiveness in the global economy, *cultivating "more affinity in its image"* and *becoming a "more appealing force in morality"*.[3] The articulation conveyed efforts at blending strength and goodwill. Indeed, the "soft" tenor of China's foreign policy has been accompanied by hard postures from time to time. This was evident during the celebration in September 2015 for marking the 70th anniversary of victory in the Chinese People's War against Japanese aggression. President Xi reaffirmed on the occasion that "China will remain committed to peaceful development", and that "no matter how much stronger it may become, China will never seek hegemony or expansion".[4] These assurances were conveyed in the backdrop of a dazzling demonstration of China's military might to the domestic as well as the international audience.

While Beijing's pursuit of power conforms to the realist (political realism) school of thought that explains international relations in terms of "power", its repeated efforts to "reassure" the world about its peaceful rise has drawn explanations from the Game Theory.[5] The practice of reassurance has been considered critical since the times of Deng Xiaoping[6] for reducing the apprehension and insecurity that has accompanied its rapid rise, and is being increasingly perceived responsible for escalating tension and provoking miscommunication between China and its neighbours on the one hand, and the extra-regional actors on the other. The "Game of Reassurance" has been devised to search for effective means of communicating positive and defensive intentions to challengers and would-be challengers particularly in the region.

China's ascendancy at the world stage has been heavily facilitated by its economic modernisation and reforms which began in December 1978. Since then Beijing has been continuously engaged in developing policies and strategies for sustaining a high rate of economic growth and improvement in the living standards of its people. The Chinese leadership is well aware that a peaceful environment is an essential prerequisite for maintaining economic progress and is mindful of the importance of crafting the national foreign policy in line with the agenda of "economic prosperity" and "well-being" of its people. During a major policy study conference organised in October 2013, soon after his election as President in March 2013, Xi Jinping underlined some of the core visions and principles of China's foreign affairs, including the "period of strategic opportunity" through 2020 for continued growth and development.[7] The Forum on *Chinese diplomacy towards its periphery* in the same conference articulated the leadership's endeavour to "enhance political goodwill; deepen regional economic integration; increase China's cultural influence; and improve regional security cooperation"[8] for projecting China's image as a global and regional leader in a subtle but convincing manner. The Forum was attended by many prominent Chinese leaders including the entire Standing Committee of the Politburo, various organs of the Central Committee, State Counsellors, the leading core group with responsibility for foreign affairs, and Chinese ambassadors to important countries for better management of relations with the periphery and resolving existing problems[9] that were seen as forces that could constrain China's rise.

The "China Dream" discussed in Chapter 2 – first articulated by President Xi in his inaugural address in March 2013 – also reflects similar objectives discussed earlier. The formulations of a "harmonious worldview", a "good neighbour policy"[10] and a "community of common destiny"[11] by the Chinese leadership from time to time signals the importance attached to achieving peace for furthering its economic agenda that would facilitate its ascent on the world stage. With economic goals the fundamental objectives and possibility of a hostile international system blocking these goals, cultivating a peaceful external environment is a policy priority for the Chinese leadership. In this respect, Southeast Asia is a testing ground for the exercise of power and practice of reassurance that by extension elsewhere can catapult the Middle Kingdom into the great-power league and guarantee its reemergence. It is therefore hardly surprising that the Chinese leadership strives to make neighbours "more friendly in politics and economically more closely tied to us" while treating them as friends and partners by making them feel safe and helping them to develop.[12]

This chapter primarily seeks to examine Beijing's attempt at regionalisation and multi-country diplomacy for foreign policy outreach with Southeast Asia in an effort to project itself as a constructive and responsible power in the region. The chapter will also focus on China's various soft power efforts like high-level visits, economic engagement and the "One Belt, One Road" (OBOR) initiative[13] or the Belt and Road Initiative (BRI) for a better understanding of China's grand objective of cultivating a positive and strong image in the region.

China, Regionalisation and Multilateral Diplomacy

In ancient Chinese foreign policy, the concept of "region" strictly did not exist. However, the term *tianxia*, commonly translated into English as "all under heaven", did figure. The translation does not imply that the Chinese rulers considered themselves *"overlords of the tianxia"* intending to rule the entire world;[14] instead the reference is mainly to the adjacent areas of the Chinese empire with which the rulers interacted regularly – namely the Northeast, Southeast and parts of Central Asia. Ancient China's Sino-centric worldview and its history of self-sufficiency discouraged imperial rulers from forming interstate alliances or groupings. The attempt, instead, was to socialise foreign rulers into accepting the Chinese empire's centrality and superiority and build a Sino-centric international order.[15] Historically, therefore, China was unfamiliar with the concept of regionalisation leading modern China to reject regionalisation as a framework for cultivating influence and building a benign image. However, the turn of history[16] and China's reluctant interaction with the world marked its break from isolationism, forcing it to open its economy and embrace both regionalism and multilateral diplomacy.

An image make-over was a critical component of China's foreign interactions even during the early years of its inception as a Republic. While distinct efforts at regionalisation for communicating a benign image took a while to take off, the projection of a benevolent non-threatening demeanour at the Bandung Conference in April 1955 attests to China's early image-building efforts through large multilateral forums.[17] China articulated two major policy initiatives at the Bandung Conference for projecting positive intentions: the Five Principles of Peaceful Co-existence[18] and a promise to negotiate dual nationality with the Southeast Asian countries for the overseas Chinese. The latter highlighted the Chinese leadership's commitment towards state-to-state relations based on mutual respect and non-interference[19] – one of the Five Principles of Peaceful Co-existence.

While nascent efforts at image-building by the Chinese leadership were underway, including pronouncing a benign intent at Forums like the Bandung Conference, regional perceptions towards China remained mixed. Indeed, prominent actors from Southeast Asia refrained from including China in evolving regional arrangements. However, over time, with China's rapid economic rise from the 1980s, the region was forced to re-consider its decision to keep China away from regional frameworks. On the Chinese side, its "forced" isolation post-Tiananmen Square in 1989[20] also necessitated the leadership to change its outlook on regionalisation. Ever since, China has been struggling to demonstrate its earnestness at regionalisation efforts to ensure stability and security for achieving greater economic development, similar to the Western understanding.[21] However, while the long-term objectives between the Western and the Chinese perceptions of regional organisations are largely similar, there is one major difference between the two with respect to region-building strategies. While the former prioritise compliance with norms such as "do as I say" and "not as I do", the latter emphasises the practice of "do as I do", thus underlining "respect for the partner" and the practice of doing together[22] – thus setting an example and stressing cooperation with the other countries.

China and ASEAN

While China was learning to respond to regional forums essentially pushed by realpolitik considerations, according to Yong Deng, China had seriously thought of joining regional institutions as early as the 1980s,[23] even before the Tiananmen Square incident. However, it took some time before China finally joined the ASEAN after being invited by the countries in Southeast Asia.

The ASEAN had already been formed providing an institutional expression to an essentially "declaratory" regionalism that had originated from the political will of the Southeast Asian policymaking elites.[24] Despite its proximity to Washington, the ASEAN decided to invite China[25] as a full dialogue partner in 1995. The ASEAN had its own reasons for inviting its big neighbour. As China made its presence felt in the region economically and its power became more pervasive, it altered the Southeast Asian countries' perception of their neighbour with ASEAN's ties with China being regarded as an imperative for its regional standing.[26] China, on its part, adopted a multiple strategy to not only end the diplomatic isolation thrust on it by the West after the Tiananmen Square incident, but also for confidence-building as suggested by Wu Yongnian, since joining the ASEAN meant little additional economic or strategic advantages for China at that point of time.[27] Southeast Asia was seen as a comfortable partner with which Beijing could upgrade and improve its association in the face of Western onslaught, given that several Southeast Asian countries are NATO members or allies and engaging them would help in conveying its positive intent to the West. These drivers were partly responsible (there were other factors as well discussed in Chapter 2) for China's "cautious" attendance of the ASEAN Ministerial Meeting in 1991 for the first time at the request of Malaysia. Thus began China's efforts at regionalism for meeting several challenges with specific agendas. Jeremy Paltiel explains China's change of position on regionalism aptly arguing that "Chinese regionalism and multilateralism far from some kind of conscious "grand design" grew out of "pre-emptive participation" designed to guarantee China's status, exclude Taiwan's political inroads and reassure neighbours".[28] Many scholars also believe that China welcomed the regional forum in order to counter attempts by regional actors to stem its re-emergence through demands for "westernisation" and "transformation".[29]

Amitav Acharya and Alastair Johnston explain the reasons behind the Southeast Asian countries' decision to include China within the fold of the ASEAN: to "engage China and integrate it into a system of regional order, thereby reducing the need for provocative strategies of 'containment'". This ASEAN strategy has been demonstrated as recently as the ASEAN Foreign Minister's Meet in March 2017 where the ASEAN discourse on the South China Seas kept to the "soft and safe" position reflecting "a cautious and restrained approach since ASEAN is navigating through uncertain regional geopolitics and all ASEAN claimant states are seeking to improve bilateral relations with China".[30] The Southeast Asian countries are unwilling to "upset" China because they are unsure how the US administration will approach the issues involving the South China Sea. It is at this point that Cheng-Chwee Kuik's thesis of the "essence of hedging" argument can be highlighted to denote a combination of overlapping rationales: while there is evidence of consensus amongst the Southeast Asian countries to engage China, their military strategies reflect a sense of defiance among and between the ASEAN neighbours.[31] However, the ASEAN regionalism has also been reckoned by Weatherbee as promoting "soft" regionalism[32] "by binding together nations on both sides of the Pacific in a cooperative framework, most notably via APEC".[33] Its further pointed out that the ASEAN's "unique convening power for bringing together the big powers of the region in a neutral setting" play a critical role in solving regional and global problems.[34]

Coming back to China's embrace of a regional forum like the ASEAN, while the effort was largely to convey China's resolve to actively participate, demonstrate restraint, offer reassurance, open markets, foster interdependence, create common interests, and reduce conflict (*jiji canyu, biaoshi kezhi, tigong baozheng, kaifang shichang, cujin xianghu yicun, chuangzao gongtong liyi, and jiangdi chongtu*),[35] the association also demonstrated the leadership's determination to offer a different narrative for practising regionalisation. The then Chinese Prime Minister Li Peng's pronouncement in 1993 that "active development of beneficial and friendly relations with neighbouring states, in striving for a peaceful and tranquil surrounding environment, is an important aspect of our country's foreign affairs work" underlined China's evolving regionalisation strategy in the context of its economic development, which while aimed at ending its political isolation attempted to do so by subtly advancing mutual development of the region. A peaceful external environment was necessary for enabling China to focus attention on economic and domestic reforms. The intent has been accompanied by necessary actions, though not always with desired results. In the meantime, with India and Japan as members of the ASEAN, China is to an extent balanced by these two players and sometimes at the behest of the Southeast Asian countries.

In 1996, Beijing signed military confidence-building pacts with Russia, Kazakhstan, Kyrgyzstan and Tajikistan, marking its initiation with the regionalisation in Asia. The following year, the First ASEAN-China Informal Summit was held in Kuala Lumpur, Malaysia, with the leaders announcing the establishment of a 21st century-oriented partnership of good neighbourliness and mutual trust, thus indicating that China had evolved as an "enthusiastic initiator" from a "reluctant participant".[36] Over time, Southeast Asia has become an important part of China's regionalisation efforts, in addition to similar efforts in Central Asia, Africa and Latin America that are aimed at improving its national image, promote economic interest, enhance national security and acquire "the power to avoid conflict" by building trust, develop collaborations and avoiding hostility.[37]

There are more academic perspectives on China's regionalisation efforts. Apart from participating in regional forums for allaying fears of other countries in the region about its rise, Beijing is also keen to "make friends in every quarter, trade goods, learn from each other and enjoy respectful interactions" (*guang jiao pengyou, hutong youwu, bici xuexi, li shang wang lai*). Some scholars argue to the contrary and suggest that for Beijing, countering the US-domination of Southeast Asia has been the overarching objective behind its regional engagement. The argument posits the Chinese leadership visualising association with the ASEAN framework as a form of "soft" counter-hegemony, involving alignment with secondary powers[38] for limiting the US power.[39] In a related argument, Li Mingjiang suggests that Beijing's willingness to involve with regional organisations is driven by its own necessity. Cooperating through regional forums like the ASEAN is perceived by other countries as China's effort to project itself as a "benign" actor with the perception enabling China to compete effectively with other major actors (especially the US) in the region.[40] Kurlantzick reflects a similar opinion: "Beijing eventually may want to shift influence in Southeast Asia away from Washington"[41] thereby perhaps adding a "hard" component to China's regionalisation efforts.

More perspectives from other scholars interpret the Chinese regionalisation strategy as neither benign nor threatening, but as an interactive approach. Callahan, for example, sees China re-emerge as a different kind of a hegemon preferring to be "status quo" rather than "revisionist".[42] The view reflects academic perceptions of China imbibing behavioural norms with an Asian mindset that inspires regional powers to respect each other's sovereignty and refrain from interfering in each other's domestic affairs. Contrarian and relatively pessimistic perceptions on the other hand note the vulnerability of Southeast Asian countries to uncertain currents of the global economic system combined with their inabilities to restrain a rising China. These views envisage China as a "revisionist" power striving for regional dominance by using Southeast Asia as a springboard.[43] Kurlantzick contributes to the pessimism by opining that China would satisfy its "own interests first"[44] through regional forums like the ASEAN while Kang feels that the countries in the region are too small to balance China leaving enough room for Beijing to expand its presence militarily.[45]

China and ASEAN: Mixed Perspectives and Way Ahead

Notwithstanding the prevalence of contrasting views, China has been integrating deeper with Southeast Asia as it is doing in regional arrangements elsewhere in the world.[46] This has led the earlier international perception of China as a "regional power without a regional policy" during the early 1990s to change substantially. While some argue that China's attitude of cooperation evidenced through working with regional and multi-country frameworks is in pursuit of a strategy enabling its ascendance,[47] David Shambaugh suggests the contrary. He argues that by improving ties with the ASEAN, China has chosen to compromise its own sovereign interests for the sake of engagement in multilateral frameworks and for the pursuit of greater regional interdependence.[48] In this context, Beijing's engagement with the ASEAN also reflects the leadership's urge to employ soft power:[49]

> Engagement with ASEAN reflects an increased appreciation by China of the importance of norms and "soft power" in foreign policy. Chinese print media, television, music, food and popular culture are disseminating across Asia at an unprecedented level. China's growing appreciation of soft power is also evident in its efforts to popularise Chinese culture throughout the region. At the same time, China also makes an effort to train future generations of intellectuals, technicians and political elites around the world in its universities and technical schools. China increasingly sees higher education as an instrument of foreign policy.

A deeper engagement between China and Southeast Asia has led China to endorse the ASEAN framework and become a founding member of the ARF[50] – a region-wide security forum (which resulted in the enunciation of a "new security concept" in the late 1990s), and active involvement in the Asia-Europe Meeting (ASEM), "ASEAN+3" and the EAS, apart from an ambitious economic cooperation project that culminated in the ASEAN-China FTA (ACFTA) which came into force in 2010. China's accession to the ASEAN Treaty of Amity and Cooperation in October 2003 as the first non-ASEAN state underlined the realpolitik streak in the Chinese strategic thinking whereby it accepted ASEAN's principles of respect for sovereignty, non-interference in internal affairs and the Code of Consensus in reaching decisions on matters of mutual interest.[51] Indeed, China's articulation of the "new security concept" indicated, among other things, the leadership's choice of a multipolar global structure characterised by broad participation in search of peace and cooperation,[52] which was in line with its broader national agenda. This was followed by revisions in China's national security strategy in 1993 that resulted in an expanded definition of security by including political, economic, defence and diplomatic priorities within its fold.[53] The objective was to elevate security on par with "high politics" while seeking an interrelationship between internal and external security challenges[54] for attuning policies with its national interests and goals. These new defining elements led to the creation of the "new security concept" in 1997 and were presented at the ARF held the same year in Beijing and later in Malaysia at the fourth ARF Meeting, thus laying the foundation for enhanced cooperation based on mutual respect and benefit.

A similar policy direction was also reflected in China's *Defence White Paper* of 2002: "to enhance mutual trust through dialogue, to promote common security through cooperation, and to cultivate a new security concept featuring mutual trust, mutual benefit and equality have become the requirements of the new era".[55] The 16th CPC held in the same year submitted: "In the area of security, countries should trust one another and work together to maintain security, foster a new security concept featuring mutual trust, mutual benefit, equality and coordination, and settle their disputes through dialogue and cooperation and should not resort to the use or threat of force".[56] The regional COC in the South China Sea signed by China and ASEAN at the sixth China-ASEAN Summit (10+1)[57] in November 2002, represents an important advance in Chinese security thinking that gives primacy to cooperation and multilateral security dialogue as opposed to military alliances, as envisaged in the "new security concept" and later the *Defense White Paper*. At the February 2017 ASEAN Foreign Ministers Retreat, China announced its plan to work with the ASEAN to complete a framework of the COC by mid-2017.[58]

While joining the ASEAN contributes to Beijing's efforts at regional image-building through cooperation based on trust and mutual benefit, it also helps meet other goals, both economic and strategic – the latter including traditional and non-traditional security.[59] Through the ARF, Beijing is able to prioritise its own development as well by focusing on five areas, namely agriculture, information and communications technology, human resource development, the development of the Mekong Basin and augmenting investment flows between China and the ASEAN. Given its geographic location, dominating the headwaters of the Mekong river, its plan to build a "cascade" of eight dams on its part of the water is sure to impact irrigation, transport and fishing for all the countries located downstream.[60] Therefore, playing a constructive and responsible role within the ASEAN can go a long way in ensuring China's economic development without irking regional anxiety. Indeed, the ASEAN platform provides China with a forum for constructive engagement of the region. While China's economic engagement with the ASEAN group of countries has been increasing over the years, such engagement is relatively more with the higher-income economies of the region like Singapore, Malaysia and Thailand. However, the ASEAN framework has also been utilised by China for reaching out to the poorer nations in the region. With economics being the cornerstone of its external relations, particularly with neighbours, initiatives like the China-ASEAN Investment Bank established in 2009 have helped China in projecting a largely "constructive" image in the region.

However, China needs to do much more to be recognised as a responsible stakeholder in the region. As the world's second-largest economy and the largest in Asia, China is among the major trade partners for ASEAN countries,[61] but is yet to match Japan, Europe and the US in investments in the region. On trade, Shen points out, "sound China-ASEAN economic relationship in future will depend on how fast China can...trim down its foreign trade competition with ASEAN economies and how much more the Chinese market can take in

ASEAN's own products".[62] There are still other opinions that are more favourable towards China and its engagement of ASEAN countries, particularly the low-income ones. For example, Cheow suggests that "with the less-developed ASEAN economies, it appears that China's trade strategy is to facilitate a quick development...especially of Indochina, so as to promote social and economic stability in China's "southern periphery"[63] namely Vietnam, Laos and Cambodia." While both views coexist, there is no denying that Southeast Asian countries continue to be concerned over China's influence. Despite Beijing's distinct efforts to emerge as a positive player keen on shaping regional behaviour and demonstrating a responsible conduct, major disagreements continue to prevail between the ASEAN and China over contentious issues like the South China Sea raising questions about China's real intentions behind cultivating a positive image in the region.

China's ban on banana imports from the Philippines in 2012 citing health protection is an example of its hard attitude that prevents its recognition as a responsible regional actor. The ban was actually a Chinese reaction to the hostile Philippines posture on the China-Philippines territorial disputes.[64] The Philippines was even accused by China for using the ASEAN meetings as a platform to hype China's land reclamation activities in the South China Sea in August 2015.[65] Similarly, the Chinese delegation at the ASEAN Defence Senior Officials' Meeting Plus (ADSOM Plus) declined the proposal by the AMS to have the Declaration on the Conduct of Parties in the South China Sea (DOC) and the COC in the South China Sea at the discussion table of the ADMM Plus meeting, to be held in November 2015, thus underlying the gap in working level interactions between the AMS and China.

It is important to note though that old alliances more than often give way to new partnerships dictated by new priorities. China's relations with the ASEAN, looked at through the prism of its ties with the Philippines, are a typical example.[66] The China-Philippines ties have improved with the Philippine President Rodrigo Duterte choosing China as his maiden destination after assuming office in June 2016. Based on a defence treaty forged in the early years of the Cold War,[67] the Philippines and the US have had a long security partnership, which aimed to stabilise the region, apart from granting Washington a firm foothold in the areas. With China growing its assertiveness in the region, the Philippine leadership did not hesitate to initiate a unilateral arbitration challenging China's sovereignty claim in the South China Sea in 2013. The move surely had the support of the United States. However, dynamics changed with the new Filipino President taking over the leadership in Manila. The President, Rodrigo Duterte, unlike his predecessor Benigno Aquino III, has recalibrated the archipelago's foreign policy, including its approach towards China, by opening a new chapter in Sino-Philippine relations that has raised concerns about Manila-Washington ties, long considered the bedrock of the United States' foreign policy in Asia. With many visualising Washington to practice a more inward-looking foreign policy under its new President,[68] the resultant absence of an alternate security provider in Asia could make the region even more unstable with the countries uncertain of fixing major power alliances in the aftermath of a possible power vacuum left behind by Washington if it chooses to and the emergence of an all-powerful China.

Malaysia has also been showing signs of greater proximity to China with the Malaysian Prime Minister praising the Chinese leadership for creating "benefits not just for the people of our two nations but also for regional stability and harmony"[69] thereby partly vindicating China's policy of building a positive image in the region. Both the Philippines and Malaysia have also signed defence deals with Beijing while Manila is exploring a 25-year military deal allowing it to purchase Chinese weapons on favourable terms. Kuala Lumpur and Beijing have decided to jointly develop and build a littoral mission vessel for Malaysia's naval forces, signifying deeper defence cooperation between the two Asian neighbours[70] and the Malaysian leadership's realpolitik considerations. With Trump in office, and the new dynamics unfolding in the region, alliances and strategic priorities in Southeast Asia are shifting rapidly with scholars suggesting that China has been a victor as far as regional diplomacy is concerned. According to Lauro Baja, former Philippine foreign affairs undersecretary, China is not only "engaging ASEAN in a very successful diplomatic position," but "ASEAN considers what China feels, what China thinks and how China will act in its decisions",[71] though it is too early to predict the exact course that it will take in the years to come.

Sub-Regional and Multilateral Cooperation

While the regional order faces new challenges, regional economic integration remains a priority agenda for Southeast Asia. The Greater Mekong Sub-region (GMS) Cooperation was instituted to strengthen sub-regional cooperation for regional economic development. Cooperation through the GMS[72] highlights yet another interesting dimension of China's region-building efforts. While China's initiation with regionalisation began with Southeast Asia inviting China to join the ASEAN in the 1990s as its full-dialogue partner, Beijing's role in the GMS, perhaps on account of its position "as the most influential power in the GMS"[73] has been that of a leader. While China took time to endorse the ASEAN norms and guidelines, its increasing confidence as a global and regional actor has helped it in leading the GMS and shaping the evolution of the sub-regional grouping. An "outsider" to the ASEAN, Beijing is an "insider" to the GMS, indicating the choices and alliances of states for furthering national interests. An initiative that was put in motion by the Asian Development Bank (ADB) in 1992, the GMS has gained traction as a sub-regional forum with which China has deepened its engagement over the years. With an eye to develop China's southwest[74] – land-locked and underdeveloped than other parts of China – engaging the GMS has emerged a priority for the Chinese leadership. According to Professor Wu Yongnian, the GMS is more action-oriented than the ASEAN with a detailed programme.[75] For example, as far as transport is concerned, a major achievement has been the greatly improved physical connectivity in the sub-region, illustrated by the near-full completion of the transport component of the three main GMS corridors, the East-West Economic Corridor, the North-South Economic Corridor, and the Southern Economic Corridor.[76] After all, an important component of the GMS is connectivity through transport corridors. Beijing's emphasis to enhance connectivity is aimed towards constructing transport networks and land passageways linking southwest China (especially Yunnan) and Southeast Asia for mutual economic development including movement of people between China and the GMS countries.[77] In addition, given Yunnan's geographic position, the province can serve as China's face to the outside world, both economically and culturally, enabling China to more forcefully transmit its "charm" to the neighbourhood through an economically flourishing Yunnan. The relevance of the GMS for China therefore has increased over time. This got amply reflected as early as in 1997 when the leadership not only highlighted a growing mutual trust amongst the GMS member countries but placed it within the broader policy initiative of China's practice of "good neighbourliness".[78]

Keeping in mind the economic synergies with the GMS and the mutual benefits that western China and the GMS members can obtain from the grouping's economic integration and progress, China has been infusing capital and technology support for building infrastructure in the GMS countries. The GMS, in this respect, is also an effective communication channel for policymakers emphasising collaboration, dialogue and consensus as its fundamentals. China has been pushing for an inclusive and balanced development of the region[79] despite being a country in the upstream of the Mekong River.[80] It is complementing this emphasis with a cooperation mechanism with countries downstream "concerned about the implications of the dam construction upstream"[81] and "could raise the issue for consultation with countries upstream"[82] reflecting its willingness to engage in dialogue with neighbours for solving problems.

Apart from regional and sub-regional frameworks like the ASEAN and the GMS, forums such as the Xiangshan – an annual 1.5 track regional security conference initiated in 2006 – are increasingly gaining traction as platforms encouraging dialogues while emphasising "partnership" as against formal alliance systems. The Chinese leadership, by invoking "stick to the family spirit" that exist in Asia encourages the Southeast Asian countries through these forums to integrate with the larger Asia-Pacific region insisting on "inclusiveness".[83] The willingness to communicate and partner with other countries also indicates China's efforts to explore a new security structure formed around its leadership. Forums like the China-initiated Xiangshan[84] are gradually becoming significant in this regard. Though the forum is a regional security conference striving to build an Asia-Pacific security structure based on partnership (*not* alliance) by putting forth a non-Western way of building regional frameworks for security, China's intentions of leading such a security framework cannot be overlooked.[85] According to the Honourable Bob Hawke AC, former Prime Minister of Australia:[86]

> Perhaps most importantly, an initiative like this by China could become a model for the kind of cooperative, constructive leadership that all of us hope China will show in Asia as it takes – as it surely will – a larger role in regional affairs. What better way to show how a new strategic and political order in Asia could and should work, and how China could and should exercise a greater regional leadership role than to step forward on this key issue.

The forum is also projected to the ASEAN countries as a "family" effort and Beijing's employment of "ASEAN-way of handling issues".[87] While integrating the ASEAN within the larger fold is desirable for a more inclusive regional order, many scholars believe that China's main objective is to build "bridges between the many existing regional security institutions and mechanisms in which it has a significant say".[88] Similar mechanisms include the SCO (mentioned extensively by Chinese speakers throughout the Xiangshan forum), the Conference on Interaction and Confidence Building in Asia (CICA, which China is currently trying to upgrade under its presidency, extended up to 2018), and the ASEAN-centered meetings (ARF, ADMM+).[89]

While China has been involved with region-building efforts through the ASEAN, GMS and forums like the Xiangshan, it has been communicating its willingness to engage in plurilateral diplomacy at the regional level through these large groupings as well. The willingness has become prominent with the fifth generation of Chinese leaders.[90] Unlike in the past, when China was reluctant to involve in such diplomacy, as it preferred bilateral engagements, a more confident but pragmatic Beijing is actively emphasising plurilateralism as a foreign policy strategy. The traditional nomenclature used by the Chinese leadership like *national sovereignty*, *territorial integrity*, *hegemony* and *power politics* have been replaced by more plurilateral inclusive terms like *interdependence*, *globalisation*, *win-win-diplomacy*, *mutual development, common interest, shared destiny, cooperative security* underlining China's new assessment of the contemporary international system and an altered strategic thinking based on more liberal and cooperative ideas.[91] President Xi's continuous emphasis on China's need to "continue to follow the win-win strategy of opening-up and a win-win approach in *every* aspect of our external relations such as political, economic, security and cultural fields" also indicates Beijing's effort to chart new diplomacy built on the premise that the world is becoming more dependent on China and could affect China significantly.[92] Xi's statement that "we should advance multilateral diplomacy, work to reform the international system and global governance, and increase the representation and say of China and other developing countries"[93] advances China's increasing belief in regional and plurilateral diplomacy and also demonstrates the Chinese desire to steer a multipolar world comprising multiple centres of economic power, diverse cultures, political institutions and even currencies.[94]

Beijing's promotion of regional and plurilateral diplomacy is also in line with its policy of reassuring its partners and neighbours about the way it plans to employ its new-found "power" in the international system. The multilateral character of the Asian Infrastructure Investment Bank (AIIB) reflects Beijing's attempt at plurilateral diplomacy[95] – legitimising and universalising Chinese interests while taking several countries of the world along on a comprehensive path to economic development. Announced by President Xi Jinping and Premier Li Keqiang during their respective visits to Southeast Asian countries in October 2013,[96] the Chinese leadership decided to expand the AIIB's membership from just Asian members to include European, African and Latin American countries as Prospective Founding Members (PFMs).[97] China even decided to drop the "aid" focus of the Bank agreeing to make it a Multilateral Development Bank (MDB) with China playing a large but not a dominant role.[98] The AIIB reflects China's desire to project a cooperative streak for pegging itself as a global leader ready to walk with the others.[99]

Another Chinese attempt at prospective multilateral diplomacy is the OBOR[100] announced by President Xi in 2013. A grand proposal to construct massive new networks connecting East Asia with Europe, it is a plan to re-position China as the world's economic centre of gravity in the 21st century. While a new diplomatic initiative, the project also underlines the Chinese leadership's deftness at employing certain parts of history for communicating its benign intentions[101] – underway ever since Beijing realised the international anxiety that has accompanied its "rise" and its need to communicate a historical non-belligerent position. The most recent effort has been to project the initiative as symbolising *communication* and *cooperation* not only within the region but Asia and the West capturing the "ancient" Silk Road spirit of "peace and cooperation, openness and inclusiveness, mutual learning and mutual benefit". A quote by a Professor of Chinese History at the Yale University, Valerie Hansen, in an article titled "China's Great Game: Road to a New Empire," very appropriately mentions China's Silk Road as a soft power initiative by the Chinese imperial rulers: "It is one of the few terms that people remember from history classes that does not involve hard power ... and it's precisely those positive associations that the Chinese want to emphasise".[102] China is perhaps attempting to reshape a new Western perspective on it through a Chinese initiative such as the OBOR. In an attempt to resurrect the ancient spirit, China also pushes public diplomacy through the initiative. The Chinese leadership is projecting the OBOR as a public diplomacy strategy aimed at consolidating the commitment of countries to the initiative. China has announced scholarships to students from countries along the BRI for "cultivating business synergies between China and their countries as most of them study finance, communications, transport and other applied sciences and management in China and move on to corporate or industrial careers".[103] These large-scale education-oriented public diplomacy efforts not only ensure a greater political legitimacy of the BRI but also fetches more strategic dividends for China. China, in turn, is able to use its financial power for getting infrastructure projects going along the BRI, and also utilising the initiative for projecting its image as a power which is reaching out to the people through education by putting a premium on it.

The global summit – Belt and Road Forum for International Cooperation in May 2017 – held by the Chinese government under the aegis of the National Development Reform Commission's (NDRC)

China Center for International Economic Exchanges (CCIEE), NDRC's top think tank – was another endeavour at plurilateral diplomacy, similar to the Xiangshan discussed earlier. Through the Forum, the leadership has been increasingly focusing on its "constructive" and "responsible" image while projecting its intent for co-development, especially with the economically underdeveloped nations: "the boost to trade will be particularly significant for the least-developed emerging markets along the route, which include some of the least-integrated countries in the world", thus targeting countries like Bangladesh and Pakistan (in South Asia), and Cambodia, Laos and Myanmar (in Southeast Asia).[104] The emphasis on these particular countries in the neighbourhood also indicates China's long-term strategic interests in the region.

Maritime cooperation with the ASEAN countries is also high on the agenda of the Chinese leadership. President Xi Jinping in his speech to the Indonesian Parliament in October 2013 promised that "China will strengthen maritime cooperation with ASEAN and vigorously develop maritime partnership with them to build the Maritime Silk Road of the 21st century", thus indicating Beijing's commitment to uphold the Five Principles of Peaceful Coexistence,[105] while conveying a non-threatening and cooperative Chinese posture to its neighbours. The Maritime Silk Road Initiative – an integral part of the OBOR – is perceived to be an attempt by China to strengthen relations with South and Southeast Asia, central to China's broader great-power ambitions, with an emphasis on maritime trade security. Professor Zhang Yunling, who considers maritime trade security a part of China's "pivot to the West" for addressing domestic development inequalities between its thriving eastern coastal regions and the economically backward and struggling western provinces,[106] views it as a "grand strategy". Wang Zheng, another Chinese critic on conventional international relations theory and an advocate of geopolitics, argues that the emergence of geopolitical economy will mark the end of international theories based on competitive mentality focusing instead on global governance marked by international cooperation and leadership.[107]

While the BRI has been projected as a grand infrastructure project with a sizeable geostrategic impact and resultant economic benefits for all stakeholders that "help promote the economic prosperity of the countries along the Belt and the Road and regional economic cooperation, strengthen exchanges and mutual learning between different civilisations, and promote world peace and development",[108] many parts of the Southeast Asian region, deficient in infrastructure, have as a result, been receptive to China's BRI for overcoming obstacles to their economic development and meaningful regional integration. Many Southeast Asian countries such as Thailand, Indonesia, Laos, Malaysia and the Philippines have already signed up substantial road and railway projects with Beijing enhancing communication, cross-border trading and the movement of people.[109]

However, there also seems to be some kind of a domestic apprehension over its feasibility. Chinese scholars like Xue Li and Xu Yanzhuo have focused attention towards deficient Chinese foreign policymaking which they feel suffers from several flaws including "laws in each step of the process: the collection and analysis of information, the selection and summary of policy suggestions, and the decision making".[110] A state councillor in China, who looks after foreign affairs, is constrained as a "decision maker"[111] given that his/her position is not amongst the top Politburo members. In addition, with no systemic mechanism for policymaking in China, the cadre and officials' relationship with the top leaders impact the eventual decisions taken. Many critics also point out that China is deploying what increasingly resembles a "debt-trap diplomacy" through the BRI, as many poorer nations in Southeast Asia would amass huge debts to China to finance the Chinese-led infrastructure projects.[112] But while certain foreign policy constraints do remain along with certain weaknesses with respect to the implementation of the BRI, China's decisiveness on implementation strategies, compared with a much slower decision-making process in India, has helped it to set off the project.[113] Further, there is little doubt that the OBOR will facilitate China's implementation of the 13th Five Year Plan (2016-20), boosting all-round reform, development and opening-up and ultimately proving to "be a linchpin to China taking on a leadership role in global trade".[114]

As China moves ahead aiming to play a more dynamic and active leadership role through the OBOR and with Southeast Asia more or less supporting the initiative, the trust deficit still remains an issue with it. Many are still concerned about China's attempt to use the grand project for increasing its relative power and making the neighbours more economically dependent on it.[115] For instance, there is a popular anger in Vietnam over China's economic dominance, "coupled with a strongly nationalistic response to maritime disputes with China" impacting bilateral economic relations between the two neighbours.[116] It is increasingly being felt that Beijing's grand Eurasian geostrategic vision (OBOR) is actually "inspired by China's rise to great power status and the transition back to structural bipolarity in the international system".[117] American political scientist Mearsheimer's argument that the interaction between powers is dominated by a rational desire to achieve hegemony in a world of insecurity and uncertainty regarding other states' intentions is what is feared by many of its neighbours.

There is also a growing fear that the OBOR may not prove as beneficial to them as it will benefit China. For example, the *Jakarta Post* in 2016 reported: "some prospective projects also could potentially be viewed as primarily benefiting China by building local infrastructure unrelated to the OBOR route, such as the $5 billion Jakarta-Bandung high-speed railway".[118] Apart from exporting China's technology and devices to these countries in Southeast Asia, Jia Limin, a Professor at the Beijing Jiaotong University, also heading China's high-speed rail innovation programme, rightly points out that it is also an endeavour to spread Chinese culture and influence.[119]

Though China is aiming to legitimise OBOR on "harmony, peace and prosperity," and trying to avoid impressions of it getting coloured as a geopolitical conspiracy for changing the existing international order, the scheme has also provoked concerns about a strategic, ecological and cultural impact of large-scale Chinese investments. Indeed, notwithstanding the scope of mutual benefit that is dominant in the discourse relating to the grand Chinese initiative, there is anxiety on part of stakeholders, as pointed out even by Chinese scholars like Zhao Hong. He notes that there are apprehensions amongst neighbours regarding China's goals from the project which extend well beyond pure infrastructure-building to garnering economic leverage that might force other countries to conform to its demands in territorial disputes,[120] quite in line with Mearsheimer's argument. Scholars like Lee Jong-Wha also argue that China "is using its growing clout to reshape global economic governance", while many Western scholars view the initiative as reflective of "China's ambitions to create a China-centric, albeit still open, Asian order".[121]

OTHER INITIATIVES

While China's participation in regional and sub-regional forums has enabled it to project its desire to collaborate and partner with neighbours, apart from conveying messages of its "peaceful rise" and willingness to engage in dialogue, high-level visits by Chinese leaders from time to time as a "diplomatic routine" or otherwise underline the importance China attaches to face-to-face diplomacy for conducting contemporary international relations (Table 4.1). Good diplomatic interaction, as many realists argue, is not only an objective of high-level visits, but are as essential in interstate competition.[122] For Morgenthau, diplomacy is "the brains of national power," which makes the various elements of national power "an integrated whole, gives them direction and weight, and awakens their slumbering potentialities by giving them the breath of actual power".[123] Constructivists on the other hand claim that signals, symbols, and persuasive tools of diplomacy, by shaping norms and beliefs about interests, can influence behaviour which is quite similar to what the Liberals claim in diplomacy, amounting to "the pursuit of joint gains through the exchange of information and arguments".[124] Regular high-level visits by Chinese leaders underline the practice of pragmatic statecraft and encouragement of dialogue, in line with what both Constructivists and Liberals indicate.

The top Chinese leadership, including the President, Premier and other high-level functionaries have been engaging Southeast Asia through multiple high-level interactions (Table 4.1), hoping to improve "mutual understanding" through appropriate diplomatic signals, sharing of information, cooperative postures and efforts to "reassure" while symbolising its new spirit of openness. According to Jen-Pierre Lehman, a Professor of international political economy who looks at

Table 4.1: High-level visits undertaken by the Chinese Leaders in Southeast Asia[125]

Chinese Leader	*Southeast Asian Country*	*Year*
President Xi Jinping	Cambodia	October 2016
Foreign Minister Wang Yi	Brunei, Cambodia, Laos	April 2016
President Xi Jinping	Singapore, Vietnam, Philippines, Hanoi	November 2015
President Xi Jinping	Indonesia, Malaysia	October 2013
Premier Li Keqiang	Vietnam, Brunei, Cambodia, Laos	October 2013
Premier Li Keqiang	Myanmar	November 2014
Vice Chairman of the Central Military Commission of the Communist Party of China Xu Qiliang	Thailand	April 2015

Source: Various Chinese Dailies and Press Releases.

China closely, and has been following President Xi's state visits in the last few years, "it is evident that no other leader has shaken so many hands in such a short time. This is China's coming out, and it's a gesture but it's also a symbol".[126] These measures are also essential for conflict management in a region where disputes over the South China Sea have generated considerable suspicion and distrust amongst the AMS *vis-a-vis* China. Managing the complex regional politics, particularly relations with individual countries and stability in the South China Sea while minimising opposition for its cause, is part of China's endeavour to strive for a positive external environment that will ultimately help shape the "China Dream" alluded to earlier in Chapter 2. The Chinese leaderships' attempt at rebuilding ties and "reassuring" neighbours is discernible from the high-level visits by the President that are also part of Xi's "major-nation initiative" launched after he assumed office in 2013.

Xi's visit to Cambodia in October 2016 and Foreign Minister Wang Yi's tour of Brunei, Cambodia and Laos a few months earlier were geared to partly court support for China's territorial claims in the South China Sea and specifically thank Cambodia for blocking the statement against Beijing in July 2016. The Southeast Asian countries failed to agree on adopting a common position on maritime disputes in the

South China Sea after Cambodia blocked any mention to an international court ruling against Beijing on maritime dispute.[127] Xi's high-level visit to Cambodia, apart from reinforcing friendship with an old friend,[128] was also aimed at expanding a long-term partnership by offering soft loans, announcing existing investments and cancelling debts. Cambodia, on its part, is also keen to figure within the larger OBOR network which could bring it positive economic dividends as pointed out by Vannarith Chheang, a Cambodian scholar: "OBOR presents a great opportunity for Cambodia to get access to financial resources and technical expertise in developing and connecting its roads, rails, and ports with the region" for increasing its competitiveness and securing benefits from the upcoming AEC.[129] Similarly, President Xi's visit to Hanoi in November 2015, the first since he took over the reins of the government, was a calculated effort to mend cracks in the relationship and "reassure" its neighbour by committing to a broad agenda of economic development. The visit and the assurance was significant given Vietnam's strained ties with China over the latter's reclamation work near the contested Spratly Islands in the South China Sea and its growing cooperation with India.[130]

Similarly, Xi's assurance to neighbours at the APEC 2013 Summit in Bali that "China will firmly uphold regional peace and stability, and help cement the foundation for a win-win situation in the Asia-Pacific" while stressing on "common prosperity",[131] highlights the relevance of high-level state visits in serving China's national interest priorities. Indonesia is also a country that seems to have been carefully chosen for announcing the Maritime Silk Road Initiative during President Xi's visit in 2013, due to several factors including its significance as an important actor in the Muslim world, a stable economy with sound long-term growth prospects and also as the largest economy in Southeast Asia and a vital country in the IOR. These factors contribute to making Indonesia one of the most important countries in the periphery with which China wants to partner for mutual benefits through the Maritime Silk Road Initiative. Having a major country like Indonesia on board in OBOR helps China in sanctifying the initiative in ASEAN, given the allure of the plan complementing the ASEAN's efforts to grow. Indeed, the OBOR and the Maritime Silk Road Initiative are winning praises in the region as initiatives that would increase regional economic prosperity while providing countries the opportunity to learn from China's successful development model.[132]

The OBOR is the latest in China's efforts to be a major stakeholder in infrastructure-building efforts in the region. China's role in regional infrastructure development is in line with an old Chinese saying : "if you want to get rich, first build roads". China is involved in some major road projects that would provide Southeast Asia land connectivity to other parts of Asia. The proposed establishment of transport corridors via Pakistan (through the Chinese-operated Gwadar Port, and then by a proposed railway to link the Sino-Pakistani-built Karakoram Highway and ultimately western China), Myanmar (through the Kyaukphyu Port then through the railway and pipeline to Yunnan, which are under construction) and Thailand (through the proposed Chinese-funded Kra Isthmus project) are some of the major infrastructure projects being scheduled under the OBOR. In conjunction with these projects aiming at unprecedented road linkages, the Maritime Silk Road Initiative, which includes an extensive network of sea and water transportation, is being seen by the region as the springboard for new economic opportunities. For a country like Indonesia, for example, the prospects imply enhanced communication between Chinese and the Indonesian marine departments leading to greater exchanges and coordination in marine policies and the possibility of establishing communication and cooperation mechanisms between maritime enforcement agencies from both sides.[133]

China's economic development assistance to Southeast Asia is also noteworthy. A large part of the economic assistance is linked to infrastructure development in the region alongside general economic aid and soft loans. China's economic assistance to the AMS is geared for augmenting its soft power reflecting in a more benign national image while securing national economic goals through greater economic integration with the region. In 2016, at a summit in the southern Chinese resort town of Sanya on Hainan island, Beijing offered US$11.5 billion in loans and credit lines to Myanmar, Laos, Thailand, Cambodia and Vietnam – the five countries along the Mekong River – for infrastructure and other projects.[134] Earlier, during the annual summit of the EAS in Kuala Lumpur in 2015, Beijing announced US$560 million to the poorer ASEAN countries, apart from US$10 billion for assisting infrastructure.[135] This followed the announcement at the EAS Summit in Myanmar in 2014, where China offered loans worth more than US$20 billion to support the Southeast Asian connectivity construction. The offer, including preferential loans worth US$10 billion for the ASEAN members and a US$10 billion special loan set up by the China Development Bank for regional infrastructure development, are major gestures reflecting Beijing's commitment to regional economic development, good neighbourliness and friendship.[136]

* * *

The reputation of the ancient Chinese traders and fishermen that they "made fields from the sea" underlines the "Chinese spirit" of adaptability and enterprise that were partly responsible for their large scale migration to neighbouring countries like Champa (central and southern Vietnam), Cambodia, Java, Sumatra (Indonesia) and Siam (Thailand) in search of livelihoods, which also led to "entangled histories". The migration ushered in a "Chinese century" in the Southeast Asian economies from around 1700 into the mid-1800s.[137] The historical emigration made Southeast Asia familiar with its "big" neighbour. In the modern era, China's strategy for diplomatic engagement of the region reflects what Thomas Schelling calls "mixed-motive games" characterised by a combination "of mutual dependence and conflict, of partnership and competition"[138] and driven by contemporary political advantages and economic benefits. However, despite strong economic ties developing between China and the region, "Beijing has found that its growing geo-economic strength does not necessarily translate into concomitant geopolitical influence and mutual trust".[139] This has necessitated a pronounced engagement of the region with greater focus on "periphery diplomacy". Beijing's practice of "periphery diplomacy" in modern times re-defines the contemporary Chinese diplomacy characterised by *cheng* (earnestness), *hui* (benefit) *qin* (closeness), and *rong* (inclusiveness) while broadening the scope of political interactions. These various characteristics of Chinese diplomacy are critical for advancing its positive image explaining the leadership's continuous emphasis on common development, enduring peace, shared destiny and win-win situation for neighbours enabling China's unimpeded progress towards achieving its eventual global stature.

China has been employing *White Papers* to articulate its vision on several aspects of national development and international engagement. The *White Paper* entitled "China's policies on Asia-Pacific security cooperation" released by the State Council Office of the People's Republic of China in January 2017[140] highlights Beijing's commitment to promote peace and stability in the region. Regional cooperation and peaceful development remain essential "for lasting peace and common prosperity in the Asia-Pacific" underlining negotiations and consultations for addressing disputes and differences.[141] Forums like the Xiangshan are also employed to emphasise their altered image reflecting China's appreciation of the "other" and the readiness to conform to international strategies of dialogue and negotiations, of course on its own terms, while taking the opportunity to pose as a leader. Beijing has not hesitated to reflect its "intolerance" in this regard, by expressing its unhappiness with New Zealand at the Sixth Xiangshan forum for "interfering" in the South China Sea dispute since it was not a party to it.[142]

The Chinese leadership has been consistently exploring ways and means to project positive intentions and display its constructive role in Asia in general and Southeast Asia in particular, which has for long been a testing ground for its exercise of power and influence. Whether it is its experiment with regional and sub-regional forums like the ASEAN and the GMS or face-to-face diplomacy combined with regionalisation and deep-rooted economic engagement, the Chinese objective is clear: recast policies towards neighbours for achieving the China Dream, a major part of which is through economic development and progress of the Chinese people. According to Hu Yong, a Chinese scholar on international relations,[143] Beijing's success within a forum like the ASEAN is not just to garner political support but also to obtain the region's "neutrality" with respect to extra-regional powers like the US and perhaps even India. Hu Yong argues, that apart from Vietnam, the rest of the ASEAN countries are not entirely "hostile" to Beijing with the Philippines aligning towards Beijing after the new leadership came to power in 2016.

While economic interdependence and the need for deeper domestic reforms have necessitated China's varied external engagement policy with its neighbours, some ASEAN countries have been equally enthusiastic for a deeper economic engagement and integration with China. This urgency to co-opt China, as noted earlier in the chapter, is perhaps dictated by history and the belief held by many ASEAN countries with "entangled histories" with China that it is better to have a strong neighbour since only then can they expect Beijing to be benevolent and find peace with its neighbours. A weak China, perceiving threats from its neighbours, might behave in a way that might be inimical to the long-term interests of the region, thus fuelling suspicion and uncertainty in an already volatile Asia encountering multiple threats and challenges.

While cooperation is defining China's contemporary foreign interactions, safeguarding sovereignty is also a major focus of the leadership underlining Beijing's hard power postures from time to time. As the discourse on "nationalism" is in vogue with China's growing economic, political and technological might, the Chinese government is showing signs of being sensitive to issues of sovereignty with people in the mainland favouring a firm handling of such matters by a strong leader in the style of Mao.[144] The leadership has been more than forthcoming in this respect. Interacting with members of the ruling CPC's inner elite in July 2013, President Xi made it clear that "in no way will the country abandon its legitimate rights and interests, nor will it give up its core national interests". There is little doubt therefore that China would continue to employ a strategy of contrasting characters towards its neighbours, one that will combine "reassurance" with firmness.

ENDNOTES

1. Yong, *China's Struggle for Status*: 3
2. Chin, 'China's bold economic statecraft': 218
3. Masuda, 'Why has Chinese foreign policy become more assertive'
4. 'China's V-Day military parade'
5. Andrew Kydd used Game Theory to develop a cost-signalling theory of

reassurance as a way to resolve the problem of mistrust in international relations.

6. Projecting a benign image overseas and shunning Mao's revolutionary stance became Deng Xiaoping's focus with economic development taking primacy.
7. Gill, 'The dynamics of US-China-Southeast Asia Relations': 18
8. Ibid
9. Swaine, 'Chinese view and Commentary on Periphery Diplomacy'
10. The working report of the 16th Party Congress in 2002 also points out that "(China) must continue to affirm to the principles of good relations and companionship, regional cooperation and consolidation of exchange and cooperation with neighboring countries." The report is also significant since it was the first time that the phrase *yilinweiban, yilin weishan*, or literally 'befriending and maintaining good relations with thy neighbor' has been mentioned, thus deepening the meaning of good neighbor policy. Finally, in the 17th Party Congress of the CCP, China's President Hu Jintao re-emphasised China's determination on realising good neighbourliness. See 'Swords in Ploughshares': 28-48
11. President Xi chose the term *mingyun gongtongti* or "community of common destiny" in Indonesia in October 2013 to express his vision of a China-centred regional community which would prosper with China's growing economic power thus highlighting co-development with its neighbours.
12. Gill
13. The OBOR is also called the Belt and Road Initiative (BRI) and has been used interchangeably in this book.
14. Kavalski, *China and the global politics of regionalisation*
15. Ibid
16. The British imperialism in China in the 17th and the 18th centuries was indeed a turn in history with the British imposing "unequal treaties" and forcing exports on China (trading China's silk, tea, porcelain for Indian opium), thus challenging and putting to an end China's dominant global position.
17. The Conference was attended by 29 Asian and African countries. See Shimazu, 'Diplomacy as Theatre: Staging the Bandung Conference of 1955'
18. The Five Principles were mutual respect for each other's territorial integrity and sovereignty, mutual non-aggression, mutual non-interference in each other's internal affairs, equality and mutual benefit and peaceful co-existence.
19. Storey, *Southeast Asia and the Rise of China*: 20
20. After the Tiananmen incident in 1989, Beijing followed a conscious policy of winning over its Southeast Asian neighbours not only to restore its regional and international image but also to evade Western-imposed sanctions. Later the 1997-98 Asian financial crisis was used by the Chinese leadership to project itself as a "responsible great power" (*fuzeren daguo*) that refused to devalue its renminbi (RMB). China's participation in the Chiang Mai initiative (currency swap initiative) and the initiation of the "ASEAN+1" Free Trade Area at the ASEAN Summit in Phnom Penh in 2002 were also geared towards projecting China's constructive and responsible image.
21. "Regionalism, in international relations, is the expression of a common sense of

identity and purpose combined with the creation and implementation of institutions that express a particular identity and shape collective action within a geographical region". See Regionalism (International Relations). Over time, many Chinese scholars have advanced regionalism as being different to the Western notion. They argue that China has insisted on the principles of state sovereignty and territorial integrity in its regionalism while positioning itself as a developing country. For details see Kavalski, *China and the global politics of regionalisation*

22. Ibid: 11
23. Yong, *China's struggle for status*: 200
24. Weatherbee, *International Relations in Southeast Asia*: 16
25. The ASEAN's expansion in the 1990s was partly prompted by the fear of China's increasing influence both at the regional as well as the global level. See Ma Y, 'Dongmeng lengzhanhou de anquan zhanlue'
26. Ma, Y, 'Dongmeng lengzhanhou de anquan zhanlue'
27. The author interviewed Professor Wu Yongnian, from the Shanghai International Studies University, in Shanghai on 18th November 2015.
28. Palitiel, 'China's regionalisation policies: Illiberal internationalism or neo-Mencian benevolence?': 49
29. Wang, 'Preservation, Prosperity and Power': 669-94
30. Hoang, 'The 2017 ASEAN Foreign Ministers Retreat: outlining ASEAN's discussions about the South China Sea'
31. Kuik, 'The essence of hedging: Malaysia and Singapore's response to a rising China': 159-85
32. Ibid: 17
33. Vogel, 'Regionalism in Asia: Why we should stick with existing structures'
34. Ibid
35. Zhang, Tang, 'China's regional strategy': 50-51
36. Kavalski, *China and the global politics of regionalisation*: 48
37. Ibid: 9
38. The main objective of the Southeast Asian countries is to keep all the major powers – including the foreign ministers of India, Japan, Russia, the US and the EU – involved in the region in an attempt to limit China's growing influence to an extent possible and to benefit from their presence.
39. Kavalski, *China and the global politics of regionalisation*: 52
40. Li, 'Cooperation for competition: China's approach to regional security in East Asia': 123
41. Kurlantzick, 'China's Charm'
42. Callahan, 'Chinese versions of Order': 749-61
43. Goh, 'Great Powers': 113-57
44. Kurlantzick, 'China's growing influence'
45. This aspect is real with China becoming more assertive in its claims over the South China Sea and the inability on the part of the ASEAN countries to bring an end to the maritime conflict. This has led the Philippines Defence Minister calling for a 'stronger commitment' from the US with respect to maritime security

and Vietnam seeking closer security ties with regional powers like Australia for consultation on defence matters in March 2015.

46. The Shanghai Cooperation Organisation (SCO) is one such initiative formed in 2001 in Shanghai, which sees China trying to integrate deeper with Central Asia (Kazakhstan, Kyrgyzstan, Russia, Tajikistan and Uzbekistan), aiming enhanced cooperation and partnerships among the member states.
47. Ikenberry, 'China's emerging institutional statecraft'
48. Kavalski, *China and the global politics of regionalisation*: 52
49. Shambaugh, 'China Engages Asia: Reshaping the Regional Order': 64-99.
50. The ASEAN had invited China to be a founding member of the ARF but Beijing was uncertain of the initiative, concerned that the US would dominate the ARF and '"internationalise" the South China Sea and Taiwan'. However, it agreed to join the Forum "out of a sense of Great Power entitlement" and to "preempt Taiwanese membership". For details see Storey, *Southeast Asia and the Rise of China*: 49
51. Yuan, *ASEAN-China Relations*
52. Shen, 'Duobian waijiao he duoji shijie': 21-25
53. Wu, 'The Chinese security concept and its historical evolution': 278
54. Thayer, *The Borderlands of Southeast Asia: Geopolitics, Terrorism, and Globalization*: 238
55. *White paper on China's National Defense* 2002
56. Kavalski, *China and the Global Politics of Regionalisation*: 51
57. The ASEAN 10+1 denotes the 10 ASEAN countries + China.
58. ASEAN's current priority is towards establishing a legally binding COC with China which would be instrumental in reducing the risk of incidents and defusing tensions not only among claimant states but also the major powers. For details see Hoang, 'The 2017 ASEAN Foreign Ministers Retreat'
59. In 2002, China and the ASEAN countries signed an AIIB declaration on cooperation in several non-traditional security areas (drug trafficking, human trafficking, piracy, terrorism, arms trafficking, money laundering, other international economic crimes, and crimes through the internet).
60. Kavalski, *China and the global politics of regionalization*
61. Economically powerful ASEAN countries have a diverse set of trading partners but poorer ASEAN countries depend heavily on China, especially as a source of imports.
62. Kavalski, *China and the global politics of regionalization*: 148
63. Ibid
64. 'China's tough stance with SE Asian countries could backfire'
65. 'FM urges South China Sea code of conduct'
66. It is interesting to note at this point that in September 2012, the Philippines had renamed the South China Sea waters off the country's west coast as the 'West Philippine Sea' which had severely dented its relations with China and fuelled discord in the region. In a little more than four years, dynamics are seen to be changing with many predicting that the US influence might wane in this part of Asia if the new administration does not take measures to win back its allies like the Philippines.

67. A Mutual Defence Treaty was forged between the US and Philippines in 1951 emphasising a mutual commitment to peacefully resolve international disputes, separately or jointly developing capacity to resist attack, and the need for consultation when the territorial integrity, political independence, or security of the United States or the Philippines is under threat of attack in the Pacific. For details see Albert, 'The US-Philippines Defense Alliance'
68. In the inaugural speech the new US President Donald Trump's assertion that 'for many decades, we've enriched foreign industry at the expense of American industry...[we've] subsidised the armies of other countries while allowing for the very sad depletion of our military; we've defended other nation's borders while refusing to defend our own; and spent trillions of dollars overseas while America's infrastructure has fallen into disrepair and decay', could destabilise the institutional edifice in the US-led global order making the US allies disconcerted.
69. Heydarian, 'Are US allies in Southeast Asia fetching to China?'
70. 'Beijing, Kuala Lumpur to develop patrol ships'
71. Calonzo, Ian, 'China scores static victory at Southeast Asian Leaders' Meeting'
72. The Greater Mekong Sub-region (GMS), rich in human and natural resource, is a natural economic area emerging as a new frontier of Asian economic growth. The area is bound together by the Mekong River consisting of countries such as Cambodia, the People's Republic of China (PRC, specifically Yunnan Province and Guangxi Zhuang Autonomous Region), Lao People's Democratic Republic (Lao PDR), Myanmar, Thailand and Vietnam.
73. 'Larger role seen for China'
74. Yunnan borders Laos, Vietnam and Myanmar.
75. The author interviewed Professor Wu Yongnian, from the Shanghai International Studies University, in Shanghai on 18th November 2015.
76. 'The Greater Mekong Subregion Economic cooperation program strategic framework 2012-22'
77. Ibid
78. Zhu, 'Mekong Development and China's (Yunnan) participation in the Greater Mekong Subregion Cooperation'
79. Premier Zhu Rongji, at the Fifth China-ASEAN Summit in 2001, proposed the development of the Mekong River basin development as one of the focal cooperative fields in China-ASEAN FTA.
80. Among the riparian states of the Mekong basin, China is the most upstream country, apart from being a political and economic superpower in the region. With a view to cooperate and for its own image-building requirement, China perhaps attempts not to exhibit its unilateral behaviour toward the lower Mekong River riparian and instead cooperates and partners the other countries.
81. China has built seven hydropower dams on the upper Mekong River (known as the Lancang in China), and plans to build 21 more. There has been a lot of concern over how these dams will impact the lives and the livelihoods of the people living in the countries downstream (Lower Mekong).
82. 'New Mekong Cooperation Mechanism'

83. Ekman, 'At the 2016 Xiangshan forum, China outlines a vision for regional security architecture'
84. The Xiangshan Forum is a 1.5 high-end dialogue platform on Asian security and defence issues. Initiated in 2006 by the China Association of Military Science, it advocates dialogue, building trust and confidence while projecting its "openness" in an effort to showcase its transformed image to the world.
85. 'Speech by the Honourable HAWKE AC, former Prime Minister of Australia, at the first plenary session of the 7th Xiangshan forum'
86. Ibid
87. Ekma
88. Ibid
89. Ibid
90. China's first generation leaders included Mao Tse Tung, while in the second generation was Deng Xiaoping, Jiang Zemin in the third while the fourth generation leader was Hu Jintao.
91. Yong, Fei-Ling (eds), *China Rising: Power and Motivation in Chinese Foreign Policy*: 161
92. Swaine, 'Xi Jinping's address to the Central Conference on Work Relating to Foreign Affairs'
93. 'The Central Conference on Work relating to Foreign Affairs was held in Beijing'
94. Chin, 'China's bold economic statecraft': 218
95. Xi Jinping reaffirmed China's position for a multipolar world at the 'Central Conference on Work Relating to Foreign Affairs: Assessing and Advancing Major-Power Diplomacy with Chinese Characteristics'
96. President Xi announced the creation of the AIIB in October 2013, before the APEC meeting in Bali. Similarly, at the 16th ASEAN-China Summit in Brunei in October 2013, Prime Minister Li announced a plan to establish the Bank.
97. Yun Sun, 'How the international community changed China's Asian Infrastructure Investment Bank'
98. Ibid
99. Ibid
100. The Silk Road Economic Belt is a project to construct land transportation corridors that connect China to Europe and all other major Eurasian sub-regions, including Indochina, South Asia and Southeast Asia. The other is the 21st century Maritime Silk Road, which is a port development initiative, targeting the maritime regions of Southeast and South Asia, the Middle East, East Africa and the Mediterranean. The two initiatives are together called the One Belt-One Road (*yidai-yilu*) initiative.
101. The exploits of Zheng He, who commanded seven voyages of trade and discovery in the Southeast and South Asian waters (1405-1433) during the Ming dynasty, is repeatedly referred to by the Chinese leadership as a symbol of China's "benign" naval presence.
102. Clover, Hornby, 'China's great game: Road to a new empire': 16
103. Palit, 'Road diplomacy: How India is isolating itself in regional space'
104. Ho, 'Connecting the Word': 8
105. 'Speech by Chinese President Xi Jinping to Indonesian Parliament'

106. Zhang, 'OBOR: A Chinese view': 8
107. Wang , 'A new understanding of geopolitical economy'
108. 'Vision and Actions on jointly building Silk Road Economic Belt and 21st Century Maritime Silk Road'
109. Ho, 'Connecting the Word': 9
110. Xue, Xu, 'The problems with China's foreign policy bureaucracy'
111. Ibid
112. Heydarian, 'Will OBOR really reach Southeast Asia?'
113. The first freight train from China arrived in Tehran in February 2016 in the wake of China's pioneering OBOR project – an ongoing investment in overland rail across Central Asia.
114. Ho, 'Connecting the Word': 8
115. There is a growing asymmetry between China and Southeast Asia's economic size since the 1990s which worries the neighbouring countries raising doubts about China's benign intentions through the OBOR. For details see Zhao, 'The maritime silk road and China-Southeast relations'
116. Zhao, 'The maritime silk road and China-Southeast relations'
117. Arase, 'China's Two Silk Roads: Implications for Southeast Asia'
118. Lingga, 'Belt and Road Summit to focus on ASEAN infrastructure opportunities'
119. 'High-speed diplomacy: Exporting China's train technology'
120. Zhao, 'China's new maritime silk road: Implications and opportunities for Southeast Asia'
121. Zhao, 'China's One Belt One Road: An overview of the debate'
122. Lebovic, Saunders, 'The diplomatic core: How the United States employs high-level visits as a scarce resource'
123. Morgenthau, Thompson, *Politics among Nations: The Struggle for Power and Peace*
124. Lebovic, Saunders, 'The diplomatic core: How the United States employs high-level visits as a scarce resource'
125. Brunei, Indonesia, Malaysia and Vietnam are four out of the seven countries in the region that have borders with the South China Sea.
126. Jing, 'Handshakes symbolise Xi's new era': 21
127. Michael, Mogato, 'ASEAN breaks deadlock on South China Sea, Beijing thanks Cambodia for support'
128. The last war China fought in 1979 was not only against the Vietnamese but was against them in defence of Cambodia.
129. Chheang, 'China is intensifying its "One Belt, One Road" initiative'
130. Vietnam renewed India's lease of two oil blocks in South China Sea for another year in 2014, just a week before Indian External Affairs Minister Sushma Swaraj visited Hanoi for more talks.
131. 'China committed to regional peace'
132. 'ASEAN diplomats welcome China's One Belt, One Road initiative'
133. 'Maritime Silk Road can bridge China-ASEAN cooperation'
134. 'China offers $11.5 billion in loans, credit to 5 Mekong River nations'
135. 'China offers $10 billion in infrastructure loans for Southeast Asia'
136. 'Chinese premier advocates peace, economic integration at East Asia Summit'

137. Lockard, 'Chinese migration and settlement in Southeast Asia before 1850: making fields from the sea'
138. Schelling, *The Strategy of Conflict*: 89
139. Zhao, 'The maritime silk road and China-Southeast relations'
140. This is the first time that a White Paper has been published on security cooperation in the Asia-Pacific which includes Northeast and Southeast Asia as well as the United States and India. For details see Singh, 'China's White Paper on Security Cooperation in the Asia-Pacific Region and Chinese Grand Strategy'
141. 'China's policies on Asia-Pacific security cooperation'
142. 'China ticks off New Zealand defence minister for raking up South China Sea dispute at the Xiangshan forum'
143. The author interviewed Hu Yong in Shanghai on 19th November 2015
144. According to a poll in 2016, the "Chinese people believe that a strong central leadership is indispensable for the rise of the country, and highly anticipate further confirmation of the role of the core leadership by President Xi Jinping during this period of historic significance". For details see 'Chinese public backs Xi Jinping as strong leader like Mao: poll'

5

Final Thoughts and Future Reflections

The Asian juggernauts – India and China – have been increasingly engaged in building a positive image for their global and regional audiences. The Southeast Asian region has been an important area for them in honing "soft" skills en route to launching the same at the global systemic. While China is an "old" player, with its rise achieving global stature and commanding awe and consternation from the rest of the world at the same time, India has a long way to go in securing such prominence. New Delhi has been taking incremental steps to connect with the world with communication gaining more traction in its foreign policy in recent years. In view of the dedicated efforts by both countries to build their images and the focus on Southeast Asia in this regard, it is important to ascertain whether their efforts have had the desired results.

While making a mark globally has been an important objective for both, their actions, particularly those of China, have generated challenges for the regional and international orders. Whether it is the Asian Infrastructure Investment Bank (AIIB), or the New Development Bank (earlier called the BRICS Bank), the Chinese objective is not only to provide more financing options for the region, but also to establish itself as an undisputed regional and a continental leader with the ability to mobilise finance for the development needs of countries effectively. The leadership agenda becomes further clear from the OBOR project that China is working on for promoting mutual cooperation for shared economic development. China's grand designs also seem to target the "old" global order wherein Western financial institutions and donors have traditionally been the sources of credit and finance, and to reform it by making it more "Asian". China's great power ambitions are matched by an equal enthusiasm on part of India as well. However, while such enthusiasm of India is yet to assume significant proportions for the neighbours and the region, China's rise is poised to rattle "established powers" in the present international order, more specifically the United States of America, compelling scholars like Martin Jacques to argue "Americans will find it extremely difficult to treat the Chinese as an equal partner...because force of habit and attitude has ingrained in them a sense of superiority and ascendancy when dealing with others...".[1]

Both the economic and strategic dimensions of China's rise have been critical in fashioning its diplomatic endeavours in the region. The former have also influenced diplomacies of regional and extra-regional actors. Classical realists have been focusing on this diplomacy as an instrument in augmenting and shaping national power for furthering national interests. The Obama administration's tact in coping with China's "rise" and its attempt to retain strategic primacy in the region involved greater engagement of the Southeast Asian countries by the US. The US President's invitation to the ASEAN leaders at Sunnylands in February 2016 for an unprecedented stand-alone meeting underscored Washington's sensitivities with the region and its "hedging" strategy for containing China. The Donald Trump administration might want to handle this in another way. While some analysts believe that his leadership could turn the US inwards and make it more isolationist, others argue that it can generate more friction and bellicosity in international affairs. A more aggressive US policy towards Beijing would definitely increase the volatility in Asia, thus, threatening peace and stability in the region. This would also imply a more troubled South China Sea adding to the anxieties of the Southeast Asian countries. Experts like Ja Ian Chong believe that "arms races and instability may become more prominent as states take to defending themselves in the absence of a credible security umbrella, and the proliferation of nuclear weapons in Asia and Europe may become a reality as states pursue robust, independent defence postures".[2]

Trump's pulling out of the TPP has also indicated Washington's aversion towards regional trade agreements as means for preserving the US presence in the region and a less-than-expected interest in staying engaged with the traditional US defence in Asia. This could encourage China to play a more proactive, if not assertive role in the region that might introduce a greater instability in the regional order triggering an undesirable rush for new partners and allies, such as the Philippines's new partnership with China as discussed in the last chapter. Washington's possible but gradual disengagement with Southeast Asia could be laying the foundation for the Southeast Asian countries being "coerced" into making choices. However, the Trump Presidency's focus on North Korea's missile programme and its need for China's support to dissipate the crisis in the region is adding yet another interesting dimension to regional politics. Thus, the US administration's vacillating and unpredictable policy posture from time to time on Asia might further prove detrimental to the region, making it even more turbulent and unstable in the process.

It is unlikely that the Trump administration would disengage from the region since such an action would be in contrast to the US concern on China's rise, which is comprehensible from scholars suggesting "if China's economic, military and geopolitical influence continues to rise at even a modest pace during this period, we will witness the largest shift in the global distribution of power since the rise of the United States in the late 19th and early 20th centuries".[3] The discomfort is pronounced given that the world's next "economic leader will be non-English speaking, non-Western, and non-democratic"[4] for the first time in centuries. The apprehension underlines the "insecurity" of the English-speaking and a considerable part of the Anglo-Saxon world and its apathy to accepting any new player (read China), from outside the "Western" domain, as a vehicle for changing the contemporary world/regional order organised by the Western powers after the end of the Second World War.

The Sixth Plenum of the 18th Congress of the CCP held in October 2016 granted President Xi Jinping the leadership "core" (*hexin*) status – granted earlier only to Mao Tse Tung, Deng Xiaoping and Jiang Zemin – underscoring President Xi's undisputed authority and drawing attention to China's engagement with the world being transformed and shaped by the continuity in leadership represented by President Xi's elevation as the "core" leader of the CCP.[5] The broader message for the global community is that the decision of the Chinese leadership is binding with no resistance to Xi's authority. This was particularly necessary at a point when the Chinese economy was showing signs of slowing down and several Chinese projects in Southeast Asia and elsewhere are being showcased as not just benefiting "the partner countries by allowing them to obtain major infrastructural improvements and industrial zones at low-interest or no-interest concessional interest rates" but also as initiatives that "will also assist the Chinese government's supply-side reform process by creating major overseas markets for Chinese industries to export their industrial plant, thereby reducing China's industrial overcapacity".[6] Fulfilling the objectives require unflinching state support that can be guaranteed only by the "core" leader who doesn't encounter opposition to his policies.[7]

Coming back to the implications of China's rise for the international order, the traditional "realist" expectation of turbulence caused by likely alterations in the existing balance of order by new actors could be a major concern for the international community. But the bigger apprehension is a shift in power and lesser concentration of actual power with its old custodians. The possibility is increasingly becoming real for the US and the Western world including Australia. Though the Chinese economy has slowed down in the recent years, there is little doubt that Beijing has weathered the global financial crisis well and continues to remain one of the most important sources for global growth. According to the 2017 Economic Survey of China conducted by the Organisation for Economic Co-operation and Development (OECD), the "Chinese economy will remain the major driver of global growth for the foreseeable future" as the country's GDP per capita remains on course to almost double between 2010 and 2020.[8] Furthermore, its significant initiatives like the OBOR are efforts to channellise China's liquidity into regional projects that would address infrastructure deficits in the neighbourhood while providing Chinese corporations and businesses returns on their investments. In this respect, the OBOR is a well-thought out plan for entrenching China's strategic influence in the region and is helping China in earning goodwill as is evident from the support received by the initiative from the region. The BRI, apart from stimulating the Chinese economy, also promises to bring Chinese foreign capital and expertise to these countries which are cash-starved and infrastructure-deficient. China invited several leaders from various countries to attend the Belt and Road Forum for International Cooperation in May 2017 including Southeast Asia. The Cambodian Prime Minister Hun Sen, Myanmar's Aung San Suu Kyi, Malaysian Prime Minister Najib Razak and the Indonesian President Joko Widodo figured in the list posing as good partners of China.

The US is not the only major global actor trying to come to terms with China's rise. The struggle is visible for major Asia-Pacific actors like Australia and Japan as well that are part of China's extended neighbourhood and countries with strong links with Southeast Asia. Australia has not only been keen to be a part of the "Asian Century" but has been eager to be a winner as well. The *Australia in the Asian Century White Paper* in 2012 was commissioned by the then Australian Prime Minister Julia Gillard to shape the nation's future course, wanting to take advantage of Asia's rise: "By 2025, Australia can be a winner in this Asian century by becoming more prosperous, more resilient, and sharing the new opportunities".[9] But it is faced with considerable strategic dilemma produced by China's spectacular rise. Australia has benefitted enormously from China's economic expansion. However, the concern of Beijing using its economic leverage to secure strategic gains is never obliterated from the Australian strategic vision. The uneasiness flows from the realisation that the regional balance of power is tilting decisively towards China from the US as it takes a firmer hold on the global economy. Australia fears "escalating rivalry if Washington refuses to accommodate China's ambitions to expand its influence in the region" since such a US posture could lead Beijing to view "Trump's presidency as a great opportunity for China to expand its role as a strategic leader in Asia".[10]

Japan, while being a major ally of the US, has exceedingly complex and nearly bitter relations with China as shaped by history. Tokyo's relations with Beijing remain strained over the disputed Senkaku (referred to as Diaoyu in China) Islands. While economic ties help in sustaining relations, Japan is naturally apprehensive of China's ambitious plans to increase connectivity and strategic influence through OBOR. In fact, many argue that India and Japan's Asia-Africa Growth Corridor has been planned for countering China's OBOR while posing as a game-changer in connectivity. Though Japan's image in the region is not all positive given its chequered history in the region,[11] Tokyo has been engaging with its Southeast Asian neighbours since the Fukuda doctrine launched in 1977.[12] A Pew Survey in September 2015 has revealed that the Asia-Pacific publics tend to view Japan most favourably.[13] Indeed, the Japan-US security alliance is perceived as critical by Southeast Asia for its security and is considered as a partnership capable of controlling China's aggressive behaviour in the region. Similarly, a proposed "Quadrilateral" Coalition on security is also underway, comprising of the US, Japan, Australia and India, and discussed amongst the leaders ahead of the ASEAN Summit in November 2017 in Manila, indicating the growing concern over China's expanding role in Asia. The leaders of the "quad" not only called for more cooperation amongst them but according to many scholars the initiative is partly to attempt a "hedge" against China's increasing insensitivity to the security anxieties of others in the region,[14] though to what extent the quad will achieve its purposes remains to be seen. However, India's inclusion in such a framework also showcases Washington, Tokyo and Canberra's intent to prop up India as a regional power while highlighting India's great-power ambitions as well.

Though it is evident that the extensive application of soft power has not negated the "rough" image of Beijing altogether in parts of the region resulting from its assertiveness, however, the Southeast Asian countries are also aware of the advantages that China brings to the region as an important player with phenomenal economic power and expertise. Beijing is not oblivious of these conflicting impressions. It continues to deploy a variety of soft power initiatives in the region – as discussed in the last chapter – for obtaining favourable impressions. China's evolving role in the ASEAN facilitating its greater participation in the regional architecture and CBMs with countries like Japan[15] underpin Beijing's urge to establish a benign image. It has been pragmatic enough to explore ways and means to "coexist" with the Asian neighbours as well as Western players without irking the "established powers". Effective soft power and diplomatic communication are essential in this respect as China pursues its quest of consolidating its status as a global player – a status it is quite close to achieving with some suggesting that China has already "emerged" as a global economic power.[16] All this has led the leadership to pursue soft power even more aggressively as a state policy. At the 19th Party Congress held on the 18 October 2017, the leadership once again reiterated its soft power policy which was seen as getting stronger improving its international image.[17] None can question ancient China's major power role in East Asia in terms of its size and history while technically and economically it was a world leader to reckon with from 500-1500. Beijing longs to reclaim its "lost" great-power status. Its soft power tools are tactical in communicating its "positive" intentions facilitating its economic rise and ascent on the world stage. China is conscious of its negative image being used for containing its strategic, economic and political rise, thereby threatening its future ascendance as well as the current international stability which it considers is a prerequisite for its eventual reemergence. As a result, China continues to work relentlessly on building its image and improving and innovating its diplomacy, while emphasising its role as a constructive player in the existing international system.

China's "benign" intent has been projected for global consumption by its leadership from time to time. The efforts are distinct in official pronouncements and documents. The report of the 16th Congress of the CCP in 2002 partly reflected this intent: "...China stands ready to develop coordination and cooperation with other countries in the field of non-traditional security issues ... to make positive contribution to the maintenance of regional peace and stability".[18] According to Alexander Vuving, "benignity" generates sympathy, trust, credibility and acquiescence,[19] thus helping an agent to relate to others without being "belligerent" or "competitive". This aspect of international relations has become greatly significant in the current world order with China appreciating the theory of interdependence it finds intertwined with its own economic development. Richard Cooper's view on interdependence from an economic point of view[20] holds ground with respect to China (with India gradually coming to terms with it). President Xi highlighted this interdependence during the APEC CEO

Summit in 2013: "China cannot develop without the Asia-Pacific and the Asia-Pacific cannot prosper without China"[21] and affirmed mutual dependence as integral to the theory of interdependence whereby it is in the interest of both agents (China and APEC in this instance) to remain engaged with each other for furthering national objectives.

Compared with China, India is still a laggard in its global and regional rise. While Huntington asserts that India is moving "into rapid economic development" and will emerge "as a major contender for influence in world politics",[22] others like George Perkovich observe it as having "enough power to resist the influence of others but still make great strides before it can attain significant power over other states, and thus, in the international system at large".[23] Notwithstanding these contrasting views, New Delhi's foreign policy activism has gained phenomenal traction under Prime Minister Modi. Since his assumption of office in May 2014, India's eagerness to harness its soft power capital for creating a better global image has been quite explicit. Beginning with the BJP manifesto, the stage for dedicated pursuit of soft power resources was set when the Prime Minister invited leaders from around South Asia to his swearing-in ceremony to signal his government's intention to begin a new cooperative chapter with neighbours. The BJP website mentions the concept of Brand India to build an Indian narrative for the 21st century as envisioned by Narendra Modi highlighting the 5Ts – Talent, Trade, Tradition, Tourism and Technology – essentially comprising the Brand.[24] Many believe the narrative has progressed from building a cult figure[25] to aligning with the national agenda of India and its development.[26]

Apart from the increasing importance attached to Brand India, more efforts are underway to recast India into a new mould by showcasing its economic progress and cultural heritage to the global and regional audience as discussed earlier in Chapter 3. As far as India's "reaching out" policy is concerned, Modi's interactions with the neighbours have been prominent. The definition of the neighbourhood has significantly expanded with the Act East Policy now looking beyond Southeast Asia and including a significant part of the Asia-Pacific. While Southeast Asia continues to remain a focus for engagement, there is an active commitment to strengthen ties with other countries like Australia, Japan and South Korea, and even smaller countries like Mongolia and Fiji. Compared with the occasional consternation accompanying China's presence in the region, India is clearly visualised as more benign. There is, however, the possibility of the Indian engagement acquiring a more substantive, including military, dimensions with the region as seen from India's possible arms sales plan to Vietnam.[27]

In the meantime both domestic and international scholars have been debating and discussing India's foreign policy under Modi: "There is little question that Modi has brought renewed vigor to India's foreign policy arena – indeed, his substantial attention to the foreign policy field has come as a surprise to most analysts of Indian politics, since during the election campaign he had evinced little interest in foreign policy issues".[28] Many experts have also been asserting that Modi's foreign policy is more Asia-focused and is different from his predecessors. While earlier efforts were "driven by the idea of demonstrating Indian leadership in a particular geography, or were manifestations of South-South solidarity, or were necessitated by security concerns emanating from across the border",[29] the current leadership's focus on Asia is different and is "designed to find partnerships, technology and funds to complete this 20th century project".[30] His "neighbourhood first" policy therefore, reflects an evolving thinking within the Indian leadership about the critical role the neighbourhood can play in the country's prosperity and development. This also, in a way, mirrors China's strategy towards its own periphery during the last several years for its own economic development, indicating the Indian leadership's inclination to learn from its neighbour. And it is also not surprising that the Asia focus and search for deeper partnerships can encourage India to play a much more involved role in the region, including that of being a security provider, as alluded to earlier.

India has also been working on connectivity projects for deeper integration with Southeast Asia. Driven by imperatives of economic development and security, coupled with the intention of playing a major power role in the region, India has been spearheading multiple connectivity projects in cooperation with the Southeast Asian countries.

These initiatives are of course lower in scale and size compared with grand projects like the OBOR. Nonetheless, Indian efforts are gathering momentum through projects implementing highways (India-Myanmar-Thailand Trilateral Highway), railway links (Delhi-Hanoi railway line) and economic corridors (Mekong-India Economic Corridor). Some Indian scholars, however, suggest that while the integration is showing signs of picking up, its benefits will not be realised unless India's backend domestic infrastructure improves.[31] Coupled with this is India's inability to deliver quickly like in the case of Kaladan discussed in Chapter 2. While the pace of many initiatives needs to pick up, it is equally true that the pace of highways and roads are seen improving under Modi's leadership.[32]

Projecting willingness to pursue an active foreign policy towards neighbours for deeper economic integration and enhanced cooperation contributes to India's image-building. Image-building has evolved as an important policy agenda for the current government. The Prime Minister's extensive travels to various parts of the world including Southeast Asia underlines the diplomatic recourse to high-level visits, seen by many as having a "global impact," and conforming to strategic application of soft power through face-to-face diplomacy. In its efforts to move towards a major-power role, India appears to prefer active and nimble external engagement strategy (as opposed to reactive and risk-averse policy) "based on a clear sense of its priorities, an integrated view of regions, and a more vigorous effort directed at confidently pursuing multiple relationships simultaneously and making a global impact".[33] This makes it clear why communicating India's future ambitions, along with the confident manner in which it has been communicated, has received large attention during the Prime Minister's visits. Modi's visit to Hanoi enroute to China for the G20 Summit in August 2016 was partly an effort to underline New Delhi's increasing strategic presence in the region, which is China's periphery and is troubled with major sovereignty issues. Similarly, India's consent to be a part of the Quadrilateral, alluded to earlier, not only implies New Delhi's activism in foreign policy, particularly with respect to its Eastern neighbours, but is perhaps a reminder to Beijing that India is no more a reluctant player in the region, ready to make hard choices, if it is in its national interest.

Both the global and regional orders are adjusting to new realities. The US, which has been a "system determining" actor with tremendous global reach, is struggling to come to terms with major powers like China and regional/middle powers like India making their presence felt globally. While India is not seen competing with the US preeminence, Beijing's rise has ruffled feathers. The two Asian giants, in the meantime, with their new-found identities as "major powers", are honing and employing various soft power tools for achieving specific national objectives. Both have focused on their status as developing countries, though the emphasis seems to have become less pronounced for China, and are working towards raising and maintaining high economic growth for sustaining improved living standards for their large populations. With both having identical goals of achieving economic greatness with strategic preeminence, their image-building efforts have been necessary and dominant. As the earlier chapters have discussed, Southeast Asia has been an important region for both countries with respect to the institutionalisation of their image-building efforts and capitalising these efforts for strategic leverage. Given the region's strategic location and resources combined with the other dynamics discussed in Chapter 2 in detail, the two neighbours are seeking to increase their footprints across the region and engaging Southeast Asia as a foreign policy priority. While China has been more proactive in this respect, largely due to historical reasons and other strategic compulsions discussed earlier, for India the region is gradually gaining prominence.

In several respects, primarily its economic achievements and the success in achieving political legitimacy for projects like the OBOR, China is well on its way to significantly amend the existing world order. The new structure might be distinct by its "Chinese characteristics", which might be disconcerting for the US and the other Western powers. But a change in the order in the manner visualised would have important contributions and lessons from Southeast Asia. Major extra-regional actors like the US are likely to continue their engagement with the region with the larger objective of limiting Beijing. India, might, over time, find itself getting more involved in the complex regional dynamics as it pursues its strategic ambitions. It must, however, tread a fine line in order to not cause further turbulence in the region.

Southeast Asia is expected to remain volatile in the foreseeable future over the South China Sea. Its important for India's own national interests to ensure that it does not let the region develop into a turf for competing influence with China. Indeed, the maturing and pragmatism needs to be as much on China's part as well. The leaderships in both New Delhi and Beijing will have to be careful in pursuing a path combining engagement and effective communication along with the preservation of long-term security interests.

ENDNOTES

1. Martin, *When China rules the world: The end of the Western world and the birth of the new global order*
2. Ja, 'What does Trump mean for Asia', *East Asia Forum*
3. Johnson et al, 'Decoding China's emerging "great power" strategy'
4. Ibid
5. Cheng-Hin, 'Xi Jinping's rise as core leader of the Chinese Communist party'
6. Ibid
7. Ibid
8. 'China remains powerful engine for global growth'
9. 'Australia in the Asian Century'
10. White, 'Australia extremely uneasy about US' future Asia policy'
11. Japan's wartime actions along with its resource exploitation and atrocities, to a great extent, have conditioned Southeast Asian' countries' perception of Japan. For details see Singh, 'ASEAN's perceptions of Japan: Change and Continuity': 276-96
12. The Fukuda doctrine articulated by the then Prime Minister Takeo Fukuda in 1977, pledged that Japan, a country committed to peace, would never become a military power and engage the Southeast Asian countries while building mutual confidence and trust.
13. Malaysians, Vietnamese and Filipinos judge Japan most positively. See 'How Asia-Pacific publics see each other and their national leaders'
14. Wroe, 'Hedging China: Australia joins security dialogue with US, Japan, India'
15. China's increased diplomatic interactions with Japan during the last few years have been noteworthy. For example, the Beijing-Tokyo Forum co-founded in 2005 by the *China Daily* and the Genron NPO is a major bilateral public diplomatic communication platform focusing on cooperation in politics, business, culture and media. For details see Palit, Sinha, *Analysing China's Soft Power Strategy*: 108
16. Wayne, 'China's Economic Rise: History, Trends, Challenges, and Implications for the United States'
17. Hu, 'China boosts soft power'
18. *China's Position Paper on Enhanced Cooperation in the Field of Non-Traditional Security Issues*
19. Vuying, 'How Soft Power works'

20. Cooper, 'Economic interdependence and foreign policy in the seventies': 164
21. 'Xi Jinping Attends APEC CEO Summit and Delivers Important Speech'
22. Huntington, *The Clash of civilisations and the remaking of world order*: 121
23. Perkovich, 'Is India a major power?': 129
24. *'Brand India'*
25. Brand Modi was created by a team of media and advertising experts who worked meticulously over the years, specifically before the 2014 general elections, and packaged, advertised and sold it to the public much like any other consumer brand. This branding has never been done by Indian leaders in the past. For details see Joshi, Gupte, 'The Making of Brand Modi'
26. Bansal, '"Brand Modi" is much more aligned with "Brand India" today: Sanjay Sinha'
27. 'India says in talks with Vietnam for first missile sale'
28. Gangly, 'Has Modi truly changed India's foreign policy?': 131-43
29. Saran, 'Watch out China: Why the "Asian century" might just belong to India'
30. Ibid
31. De, 'India's emerging connectivity with Southeast Asia: Progress and Prospects'
32. Sharma, 'Drones, satellites on the job as Modi pushes team to meet his election promises'

333. Parameswaran, 'A new 'proactive' Indian foreign policy under Modi'

Bibliography

'A Cooperative Strategy for 21st century Sea Power', March 2015 at http://www.navy.mil/local/maritime/150227-CS21R-Final.pdf (Accessed 26 June 2015)

Arase, David, 'China's Two Silk Roads: Implications for Southeast Asia', *ISEAS Perspectives*, 22 January 2015 at https://www.iseas.edu.sg/images/pdf/ISEAS_Perspective_2015_2.pdf (Accessed 9 May 2017)

———, 'China's Two Silk Roads initiative what it means for Southeast Asia' in Singh, Daljit (ed.) *Southeast Asian Affairs*, 2015, Singapore: ISEAS Publishing

Arndt, T. Richard, *The First Resort of Kings: American Cultural Diplomacy in the 21st Century*. Washington DC: Potomac Books, 2005

'ASEAN Community at the top of the agenda for 2015 summit', *Channel News Asia*, 25 April, 2015 at http://www.channelnewsasia.com/news/singapore/asean-community-at-the/1806598.html (Accessed 12 October 2015)

'ASEAN Defence Ministers Meeting Plus', *CSS Strategic Background Paper* – 03/13 at http://www.victoria.ac.nz/hppi/centres/strategic-studies/documents/ASEANPlus.pdf (Accessed 7 October 2015)

'ASEAN diplomats welcome China's One Belt, One Road initiative', *Channel News Asia*, 16 November 2015 at http://www.channelnewsasia.com/news/asiapacific/asean-diplomats-welcome/2265422.html (Accessed 30 November 2015)

'ASEAN, India to boost cultural cooperation and linkages', *Permanent Mission of the Republic of Singapore*, ASEAN Jakarta, 20 January 2017 at https://www.mfa.gov.sg/content/mfa/overseasmission/asean/latest_news_in_asean/2017/2017-01/2017-01-13 Latest News In ASEAN1.html (Accessed 17 April 2017)

'ASEAN Socio-Cultural Community (ASCC)', *Fact Sheet* at http://www.asean.org/images/2013/factsheet/2013%20(6.%20Jun)%20-%20ASCC.pdf (Accessed 12 October 2015)

'ASEAN State of Education Report 2013' at http://www.asean.org/resources/publications/asean-publications/item/asean-state-of-education-report-2013?category_id=382 (Accessed 12 October 2015)

'Australia in the Asian Century', *Australian Government*, October 2012 at http://espas.eu/orbis/sites/default/files/generated/document/en/Australia%20in%20the%20Asian%20century_White%20Paper.pdf (Accessed 11 May 2017)

Bajpai, P. Kanti, Pant, V. Harsh, *India's Foreign Policy: A Reader*. New Delhi: OUP, 2013

Bansal, Shuchi, '"Brand Modi" is much more aligned with "Brand India" today: Sanjay Sinha', *Livemint*, 21 March 2017 at http://www.livemint.com/Consumer/5hCuf02dl9yMTxoB2rG6OP/Brand-Modi-is-much-more-aligned-with-Brand-India-today.html (Accessed 21 March 2017)

Baruah, Darshana, 'Japan: India's unique maritime partner', *Asia Maritime Transparency Initiative*, 17 November 2016 at https://amti.csis.org/japan-indias-unique-maritime-partner/ (Accessed 29 March 2017)

'Beijing, Kuala Lumpur to develop patrol ships', *China Daily*, 2 November 2016 at http://europe.chinadaily.com.cn/china/2016-11/02/content_27246872.htm (Accessed 20 February 2017)

Beri, Ruchita, 'Maritime Security', *Indian Ocean Watch*, December 2012 at http://www.idsa.in/system/files/IOW_12.pdf (Accessed 17 April 2017)

Bose, Ranjan, Pratim, 'All's not quiet on the eastern front', *Business Line*, 9 March 2017 at http://www.thehindubusinessline.com/opinion/indias-intercountry-road-projects-on-eastern-front/article9577952.ece (Accessed 5 July 2017)

Brand India, BJP at http://www.bjp.org/core-issues/vision-of-modi-header/brand-india (Accessed 11 May 2017)

Brewster, David, 'India's engagements with Southeast Asia: Singapore, Vietnam and Indonesia', in Hall, Ian (ed.) *The Engagement of India*. Washington DC: Georgetown University Press, 2014

'Brief on India-Laos Bilateral Relations', *Embassy of India, Lao PDR* at http://indianembassylaos.org/eoi.php?id=Bilateral (Accessed 13 October 2015)

Calonzo, Andreo, Ian, C. Savson, 'China Scores Tacit Victory at Southeast

Asian Leaders' Meeting', *Bloomberg*, 30 April 2017 at https://www.bloomberg.com/news/articles/2017-04-30/china-scores-tacit-victory-at-southeast-asian-conclave-in-manila (Accessed 6 July 2017)

Chanda, Nayan, 'S-E Asia still important to India's development and security', *Straits Times*, 26 June 2014 at http://www.straitstimes.com/opinion/s-e-asia-still-important-to-indias-development-and-security (Accessed 28 March 2017)

Chatterjee, Shibashis, 'The Look East Policy and India's Northeastern States', *RSIS Policy Report*, March 2014 at https://www.rsis.edu.sg/wp-content/uploads/2014/07/PR140301_The_Look_East_Policy_and_India_Northeastern_States.pdf (Accessed 16 October 2015)

Chaulia, Sreeram, *Modi Doctrine*. New Delhi: Bloomsbury, 2016

Cheng-Hin Lim, Alvin, 'Xi Jinping's rise as core leader of the Chinese Communist Party', *IPP*, 29 October 2016 at http://www.ippreview.com/index.php/Blog/single/id/268.html (Accessed 20 March 2017)

Cheunboran, Chanborey, 'The South China Sea and ASEAN unity: A Cambodian Perspective', *ASEAN Studies Program* at https://thcasean.org/read/articles/268/The-South-China-Sea-and-ASEAN-Unity-A-Cambodian-Perspective (Accessed 19 April 2017)

Chheang, Vannarith, 'China is intensifying its "One Belt, One Road" initiative, *The Khmer Times*, 30 December 2015 at https://vannarithchheang.com/2016/01/01/china-is-intensifying-its-one-belt-one-road-initiative/ (Accessed 23 February 2017)

Chin, T. Gregory, 'China's bold economic statecraft', *Current History*, September 2015

'China's policies on Asia-Pacific security cooperation', *White Paper*, January 2017 at http://news.xinhuanet.com/english/china/2017-01/11/c_135973695_6.htm (Accessed 2 March 2017)

'China remains powerful engine for global growth', *China Daily*, 21 April 2017 at http://www.chinadaily.com.cn/business/2017-04/21/content_29027090.htm (Accessed 11 May 2017)

'China offers $11.5 billion in loans, credit to 5 Mekong River nations', *Asia Times*, 23 March 2016 at http://www.atimes.com/article/china-offers-11-5-billion-in-loans-credit-to-5-mekong-river-nations/ (Accessed 6 July 2017)

'China ticks off New Zealand defence minister for raking up South China Sea dispute at the Xiangshan forum', *The Straits Times*, 11 October 2016 at http://www.straitstimes.com/asia/east-asia/china-ticks-off-new-zealand-defence-minister-for-raking-up-south-china-sea-dispute-at (Accessed 2 March 2017)

'China celebrates 70 years since victory over Japan', *Channel News Asia,* 3 September 2015 at http://www.channelnewsasia.com/news/asiapacific/china-celebrates-70-years/2097252.html (Accessed 10 March 2017)

'China's V-Day military parade', *China Insight,* 10 September 2015 at http://english.cccws.org.cn/archiver/cccwsen/UpFile/Files/Default/20151009172041810810.pdf (Accessed 28 February 2017)

'China offers $10 billion in infrastructure loans for Southeast Asia', *Reuters,* 22 November 2015 at http://www.reuters.com/article/2015/11/22/us-asean-summit-china-aid-idUSKBN0TB0BA20151122#WmGfxcOkB12QzxxZ.97 (Accessed 1 December 2015)

'China's tough stance with SE Asian countries could backfire', *Vietnamnet,* 10 June 2014 at http://english.vietnamnet.vn/fms/special-reports/104613/china-s-tough-stance-with-se-asian-countries-could-backfire.html (Accessed 1 November 2015)

'Chinese Premier advocates peace, economic integration at East Asia Summit', *Xinhuanet,* 13 November 2014 at http://news.xinhuanet.com/english/china/2014-11/13/c_133788217.htm (Accessed 1 December 2015)

'China Focus: Chinese Premier reaffirms road of peaceful development', *CCTV,* 17 March 2013 at http://english.cntv.cn/20130317/103691.shtml (Accessed June 29, 2015)

'China committed to regional peace', *China.org.cn,* 8 October 2013 at http://www.china.org.cn/world/2013-10/08/content_30219733.htm (Accessed 27 November 2015)

China's Position Paper on Enhanced Cooperation in the Field of Non-Traditional Security Issues, May 2002 athttp://wcm.fmprc.gov.cn/pub/eng/wjb/zzjg/gjs/gjzzyhy/2612/2614/t15318.htm (Accessed 13 April 2016)

'Chinese public backs Xi Jinping as strong leader like Mao: poll', *The Indian Express,* 26 October 2016 at http://indianexpress.com/article/world/world-news/chinese-public-backs-xi-jinping-as-strong-leader-like-mao-poll-3103895/ (Accessed 8 May 2017)

Chopra, Ritika, 'Allow foreign university campuses, says Niti Ayog', *The Indian Express,* 16 April, 2016 at http://indianexpress.com/article/india/india-news-india/allow-foreign-university-campuses-niti-aayog-2755773/ (Accessed 3 February 2017)

Christopher, K. Johnson, Ernest Z. Bower, Cha, D. Victor, Green, J. Michael,

Goodman, P. Matthew, 'Decoding China's emerging "great power" strategy', *China File*, Center for Strategic and International Studies, June 2014 at https://www.chinafile.com/library/reports/decoding-chinas-emerging-great-power-strategy-asia (Accessed 13 April 2016)

Clark, Helen, 'Why China should fear India's arms sales to Vietnam (Think South China Sea), *The National Interest*, 11 January 2017 at http://nationalinterest.org/blog/the-buzz/why-china-should-fear-indias-arms-sales-vietnam-think-south-19025 (Accessed 17 April 2017)

Clinton, Hillary, 'America's Pacific Century', *Foreign Policy*, 22 July 2012 at http://foreignpolicy.com/2011/10/11/americas-pacific-century/ (Accessed 23 June 2015)

Clover, Charles, Hornby, Lucy, 'China's great game: Road to a new empire', *Today*, 14 October 2015

Coedes, George, *The Indianised states of Southeast Asia*. Honolulu: University of Hawaii Press, 1968

'Constructivism in International Relations' at http://international relations.org/constructivism_in_international_relations/ (Accessed 4 July 2017)

Cooper, N. Richard, 'Economic interdependence and foreign policy in the seventies', *World Politics*, January 1972

Das, Kumar, Ajay, 'India-ASEAN Defence Relations', *RSIS Monograph*, 2013 at https://www.rsis.edu.sg/wp-content/uploads/2000/01/Monograph28.pdf (Accessed 10 October 2015)

Das, Kumar, Samir, 'India's Look East Policy: Imagining a New Geography of India's northeast', *India Quarterly: A Journal of International Affairs*, 66 (4), 2010

David, Scott, 'India's "extended neighbourhood" concept: power projection for a rising power', *India Review* 8 (9), April-June, 2009 at http://www.d-scott.com/wp-content/uploads/2013/09/india-extendedneighbourhood.pdf (Accessed 1 October 2015)

De, Prabir, 'India's emerging connectivity with Southeast Asia: Progress and Prospects', *ADBI Working Paper Series*, December 2014 at https://www.adb.org/sites/default/files/publication/156362/adbi-wp507.pdf (Accessed 21 March 2017)

'Deepening Reform and Upgrading China', *Third Plenary Session of the 18th CPC Central Committee*, 9 November 2013 at http://en.people.cn/102775/208695/ (Accessed 29 June 2015)

Defence White Paper 2016, Australian Government, Department of Defence at http://www.defence.gov.au/whitepaper/docs/2016-defence-white-paper.pdf (Accessed 19 April 2017)

Defence White Paper 2013, Australian Government, Department of Defence at http://www.defence.gov.au/whitepaper/2013/docs/WP_2013_web.pdf (Accessed June 30, 2015)

Deng Yong, 'The new hard realities: "Soft Power" and China in transition', in Li Mingling (ed.) *Soft Power: China's Emerging Strategy in International Politics.* UK: Lexington Books, 2009

Denmark, M. Abraham, 'Asia's security and the contested Global Commons', *Strategic Asia 2010-11*

Dessein, Bart (ed.), *Interpreting China as a regional and global power.* NY: Palgrave Macmillan, 2014

'Development Partnership Administration' at http://mea.gov.in/development-partnership-administration.htm (Accessed 14 October 2015)

Ekman, Alice, 'At the 2016 Xiangshan forum, China outlines a vision for regional security governance', *The Diplomat,* 15 October 2016 at http://thediplomat.com/2016/10/at-the-2016-xiangshan-forum-china-outlines-a-vision-for-regional-security-governance/ (Accessed 2 March 2017)

Eleanor, Albert, 'The US-Philippines Defence Alliance', *CFR Backgrounders,* 21 October 2016 at http://www.cfr.org/philippines/us-philippines-defense-alliance/p38101 (Accessed 3 May 2017)

Farewell, P. James, *Persuasion and Power.* DC: Georgetown University Press, 2012

Faulkner, Neil, 'The official truth: Propaganda in the Ancient Roman Empire', *BBC,* 17 February 2011 at http://www.bbc.co.uk/history/ancient/romans/romanpropaganda_article_01.shtml (Accessed 8 March 2017)

'FM urges South China Sea code of conduct', *The Global Times,* 6 August 2015 at http://www.globaltimes.cn/content/935726.shtml (Accessed 2 November 2015)

Gangly, Sumit, 'Has Modi truly changed India's foreign policy?', *The Washington Quarterly* 40 (2), Summer 2017

Gill, Bates, Goh Evelyn, Chin-Hao Huang, 'The dynamics of US-China-Southeast Asia Relations, *The United States Study Centre,* June 2016 at http://ussc.edu.au/ussc/assets/media/docs/publications/2016_DynamicsOfUSChina SoutheastAsiaRelations.pdf (Accessed 20 February 2017)

Goh, E., 'Great Powers', *Information Systems* 32 (3), 2007/08

Gupta, Arvind, 'Myanmar's critical role in bolstering India's Look East Policy', 2 February 2012, *IDSA Commentary*, 2 February 2012 at http://www.idsa.in/idsacomments/MyanmarsCriticalRoleinBolsteringIndiasLookEastPolicy_agupta_020212 (Accessed 28 March 2017)

Hall, Ian, 'India in Australia's 2016 Defence White Paper', *Regional Security Comment* at https://www.regionalsecurity.org.au/resources/Documents/SC%2012-1%20Hall.pdf (Accessed 19 April 2017)

Hall, Todd, Keren, Yarhi-Milo, 'The Personal Touch: Leaders' impressions, costly signalling and assessments of sincerity in international affairs', *International Studies Quarterly*, 56(3), 2012

'Hand in Hand', *The Economist*, 1 June 2015 at http://www.economist.com/news/asia/21578714-shinzo-abe-has-compelling-diplomatic-well-economic-reasons-push-south-east-asia-hand (Accessed 30 June 2015)

'Here's how Modi has strengthened India's Navy', *Business Insider*, 15 September 2015 at http://www.businessinsider.in/Heres-how-Modi-has-strengthened-Indias-navy/articleshow/48972278.cms (Accessed October 6, 2015)

Heydarian, Javad, Richard, 'Will OBOR really reach Southeast Asia?' *Asia Times*, 17 May 2017 at http://www.atimes.com/article/will-obor-really-reach-southeast-asia/ (Accessed 18 May 2017)

_______, 'Are US allies in Southeast Asia fetching to China?', *Al Jazeera*, 8 November 2016 at http://www.aljazeera.com/indepth/opinion/2016/11/malaysia-philippines-relations-china-161107101018957.html (Accessed 20 February 2017)

'High-speed diplomacy: Exporting China's train technology', *ShanghaiDaily.com*, 9 May 2017 at http://www.shanghaidaily. com/business/benchmark/Highspeed-diplomacy-Exporting-Chinas-train-technology/shdaily.shtml (Accessed 9 May 2017)

Ho Carmen, 'Connecting the Word', *China Daily* (Asia Weekly), 1-7 May, 2017

HoangThi, Ha, 'The 2017 ASEAN Foreign Ministers Retreat: outlining ASEAN's discussions about the South China Sea', *ISEAS Perspective*, 13 March 2017 at https://www.iseas.edu.sg/images/pdf/ISEAS_Perspective_2017_17.pdf (Accessed 15 March 2017)

Hongying Wang, 'National image building and Chinese foreign policy', *Paper presented at the annual meeting of the American Political Science Association*, Boston, 2002

'How Asia-Pacific publics see each other and their national leaders', *Pew research Centre Global Attitudes and Trends*, 2 September 2015 at http://www.pewglobal.org/2015/09/02/how-asia-pacific-publics-see-each-other-and-their-national-leaders/ (Accessed 17 March 2017)

Hu Yongqi, 'China boosts soft power', *China Daily*, 21 October 2017 at http://www.chinadaily.com.cn/china/2017-10/21/content_33517509.htm (Accessed 14 November 2017)

Huntington, P. Samuel, *The Clash of Civilisations and the remaking of world order*. New Delhi: Penguin Books, 1997

'If Only Singaporeans stopped to think', 10 July 2012 at http://ifonlysingaporeans.blogspot.sg/2012/07/why-india-needs-to-take-singapore.html (Accessed 19 June 2015)

Ikenberry, G, Lim, John, Darren, J., 'China's emerging institutional statecraft', *Brookings*, April 2017 at https://www.brookings.edu/wp-content/uploads/2017/04/chinas-emerging-institutional-statecraft.pdf (Accessed 2 May 2017)

'India expects 9 lakh South East Asian tourists this year', *The Economic Times*, 5 May 2016 at http://economictimes.indiatimes.com/industry/services/travel/india-expects-9-lakh-south-east-asian-tourists-this-year/articleshow/52121776.cms (Accessed 9 February 2017)

'India is a messenger of world peace', *Mann ki Baat*, 29 October 2017 at http://www.thehindu.com/news/national/mann-ki-baat-india-is-a-messenger-of-world-peace-says-modi/article19943906.ece (Accessed 31 October 2017)

'India ranks twelfth for tourist arrivals in the Philippines', *ETB Travel News*, 5 November 2015 at http://australia.etbtravelnews.global/268619/india-ranks-twelfth-for-tourist-arrivals-in-the-philippines/ (Accessed 17 May 2017)

'India says in talks with Vietnam for first missile sale', *The Hindustan Times*, 15 February 2017 at http://www.hindustantimes.com/india-news/india-says-in-talks-with-vietnam-for-first-missile-sale/story-UTN5sF3DOTgv4FOUNRLlgJ.html (Accessed 11 May 2017)

'India's new gateway to ASEAN', *Bangkok Post*, 24 November 2014 at http://www.bangkokpost.com/print/445087/ (Accessed 15 October 2015)

India-Philippines Relations, December 2013 at http://mea.gov.in/Portal/ForeignRelation/Philippines__December_2013_.pdf (Accessed 19 June 2015)

India-Singapore Relations at https://hcisingapore.gov.in/pages.php?id=68 (Accessed 19 June 2015)

'Indian arms sale to Hanoi disturbing if aimed at China', *Global Times*, 11 January 2017 at www.globaltimes.cn/content/1028164.shtml (Accessed 20 April 2017)

'Indian Foreign Policy: A Road Map for the Decade Ahead', Speech by External Affairs Minister Shri Pranab Mukherjee at the 46th National Defence College Course, *Ministry of External Affairs*, Government of India, November 15, 2006 at http://www.mea.gov.in/Speeches-Statements.htm?dtl/2395/ (Accessed July 10, 2015)

'Indonesia to raise prospect of joint patrols with Australia in South China Sea: Report', *Asia Maritime Reviews*, 23 May, 2017 at http://asiamaritime.net/indonesia-to-raise-prospect-of-joint-patrols-with-australia-in-south-china-sea-report/ (Accessed 4 July 2017)

Iyengar, Rishi, 'India is using its military incursions into Burma to send a message of other countries', *Time*, 11 June 2015 at http://time.com/3917362/india-burma-army-operation-militant-attack-pakistan-manipur/ (Accessed 17 April 2017)

Ja, Ian, Chong, 'What does Trump mean for Asia', *East Asia Forum*, 25 January 2017 at http://www.eastasiaforum.org/2017/01/25/what-does-trump-mean-for-asia/ (Accessed 17 March 2017)

Jacques, Martin, *When China rules the world: The end of the Western world and the birth of the new global order*. USA: Penguin, 2009

Jennings, Relph, 'Vietnam takes Asia lead in figuring out Trump policy on South China Sea', *VOA*, 22 May 2017 at https://www.voanews.com/a/vietnam-takes-lead-in-figuring-out-trump-policy-on-south-china-sea/3864859.html (Accessed 4 July 2017)

Jing Fu, 'Handshakes symbolise Xi's new era', *China Daily*, 12-18 June 2017

'Joint Statement on a strategic partnership by the Prime Ministers of the Republic of India and the Republic of Singapore "renewed sprite and new energy"', *Ministry of Foreign Affairs Singapore*, 24 November 2015 at https://www.mfa.gov.sg/content/mfa/media_centre/press_room/pr/2015/201511/press_201511243.htmln (Accessed 17 April 2017)

Joshi, Devina, Gupte, Masoom, 'The Making of Brand Modi', *Business India*, 12 May 2014 at http://www.business-standard.com/article/management/the-making-of-brand-modi-114051100589_1.html (Accessed 21 March 2017)

Kang, Hyungseok, 'Reframing Cultural Diplomacy: International cultural politics of Soft Power and the creative economy', 2013 at http://

www.culturaldiplomacy.org/academy/content/pdf/participant-papers/2011-08-loam/Reframing-Cultural-Diplomacy-International-Cultural-Politics-of-Soft-Power-and-the-Creative-Economy-Hyungseok-Kang.pdf (Accessed 12 October 2015)

Kavalski, Emilian, *China and the Global Politics of Regionalisation*. USA: Ashgate Publishing Company, 2013

Keaney, A. Brian, 'The Realism of Hans Morgenthau', 2006 at http://scholarcommons.usf.edu/cgi/viewcontent.cgi?article=3579&context=etd (Accessed 22 October 2012)

Kerrey, J. Robert, Manning A. Robert, 'The United States and Southeast Asia: A policy agenda for the new administration', *Council on Foreign Relations Task Force Report*, 2001

Koh, Sween, Lean, Collin, Nagao, Satoru, 'Toward a Japan-Singapore-India maritime partnership', *The Japan Times*, 16 February 2016 at http://www.japantimes.co.jp/opinion/2016/02/16/commentary/japan-commentary/toward-japan-singapore-india-maritime-partnership/#.WNtnhmPBbVo (Accessed 29 March 2017)

Kor, Kian, Beng, 'China President Xi dismisses Hague arbitration on South China Sea but says "committed to peace"', *Straits Times*, 13 July 2016 at http://www.straitstimes.com/asia/east-asia/china-dismisses-hague-ruling-maintains-sovereignty-over-south-china-sea (Accessed 8 May 2017)

Kugelman, Michael, 'India acts East', *Foreign Policy*, May 17, 2016 at http://foreignpolicy.com/2016/05/17/india-acts-east/ (Accessed 20 February 2017)

Kuik, Ch., 'The essence of hedging: Malaysia and Singapore's response to a rising China', *Contemporary Southeast Asia* 30 (2), 2008

Kumar, Rajiv, 'Why India-Vietnam ties are important?' 29 October 2014 at http://www.dailyo.in/politics/why-india-vietnam-ties-are-important/story/1/498.html (Accessed 19 June 2015)

Kurlantzick, Joshua, 'China's Charm: Implications of Chinese Soft Power', *Carnegie Endowment for International Peace* PolicyBrief#47, June 2006 at http://carnegieendowment.org/files/PB_47_FINAL.pdf (Accessed 13 March 2017)

______, 'China's growing influence' in Roett, Riordan and Paz, Guadalupe (eds.), *China's Expansion into the Western Hemisphere: Implications for Latin America and the United States*. Washington: Brookings Institution Press, 2008

Lai Hongyi, Lim Tin Seng, *Harmony and Development: ASEAN-China*

Relations. Singapore: World Scientific Publishing Co. Pte. Ltd, 2007

'Larger role seen for China', *China Daily*, 19 December 2014 at http://www.chinadaily.com.cn/world/2014livisitkst/2014-12/19/content_19121343.htm (Accessed 12 November 2015)

Lebovic, H. James, Saunders, N. Elizabeth, 'The Diplomatic Core: How the United States employs high-level visits as a scarce resource', March 2014 at http://www.isanet.org/Publications/ISQ/Posts/ID/5040/The-Diplomatic-Core-The-Determinants-of-High-Level-US-Diplomatic-Visits-19462010 (Accessed 13 March 2017)

Leur, JC Van, 'On Early Asian Trade' in Leur, Van (ed.), *Indonesian Trade and Society: Essays in Asian Social and Economic History*. The Hague: W.van Hoeve Ltd, 1955)

Li Mingjiang, 'Cooperation for competition: China's approach to regional security in East Asia' at https://www.rsis.edu.sg/staff-publication/cooperation-for-competition-chinas-strategic-response-to-us-supremacy-in-east-asia/#.VjmNZ03ov4g (Accessed 4 November 2015)

Lingga, Vincent, 'Belt and Road Summit to focus on ASEAN infrastructure opportunities', *The Jakarta Post*, 19 April 2016 at https://www.pressreader.com/indonesia/the-jakarta-post/20160419/281728383691057 (Accessed 8 May 2017)

Lintner, Bertil, 'India-ASEAN Economic Relations', *Far Eastern Economic Review*, November 2006 at http://www.asiapacificms.com/articles/india_asean_relations/ (Accessed 29 March 2017)

'List of ICCR operational Hindi Chairs' at http://iccr.gov.in/sites/default/files/list%20of%20chairs.pdf (Accessed 30 March 2017)

Lockard, A. Craig, 'Chinese migration and settlement in Southeast Asia before 1850: making fields from the sea', *History Compass*, 4 September 2013 at http://onlinelibrary.wiley.com/doi/10.1111/hic3.12079/abstract (Accessed 2 March 2017)

Lustick, S. Ian, 'The absence of Middle Eastern Great Powers: Political "Backwardness" in historical perspective', *International Organisation* 51, Autumn 1997

Lyon, Rod, 'The Southeast Asian emphasis in DWP 2013', *The Strategist*, 21 June 2013 at https://www.aspistrategist.org.au/the-southeast-asian-emphasis-in-dwp2013/ (Accessed 25 September 2017)

Ma Y, 'Dongmeng lengzhanhou de anquan zhanlue' (ASEAN post-Cold War era's security strategy) in Yan X (ed.) *Zhonguo yu YaTai anquan* (China and Asia-Pacific Security). Beijing: Beijing Shishi Chaubanshe, 1999

Make in India at http://www.makeinindia.com/ (Accessed 18 June 2015)

'Malaysia strategic shift towards China in a setback to US', *The Times of India*, 2 November 2016 at https://timesofislamabad.com/malaysia-strategic-shift-towards-china-set-back-us/2016/11/02/ (Accessed 21 April 2017)

Malik, Mohan, 'China and strategic imbalance', *The Diplomat*, 14 July 2014 at http://thediplomat.com/2014/07/china-and-strategic-imbalance/ (Accessed 23 June 2015)

Malone, David, 'Soft power in Indian foreign policy', *Economic and Political Weekly*, 3 September 2011 at https://www.idrc.ca/sites/default/files/sp/Documents%20EN/EPW-Soft-Power-3-September-2011.pdf (Accessed 17 May 2017)

______, *Does the Elephant Dance: Contemporary Indian Foreign Policy*. New York: Oxford University Press, 2011

Mansfield, Edward, Milner, V. Helen, *The Political Economy of Regionalism*. New York: Columbia University Press, 1997

'Maritime Silk Road can bridge China-ASEAN cooperation', *Jakarta Post*, 5 August 2015 at http://www.thejakartapost.com/news/2015/08/05/maritime-silk-road-can-bridge-china-asean-cooperation.html (Accessed 30 November 2015)

Masuda, Masayuki, 'Why has Chinese foreign policy become more assertive?', *East Asia Forum*, 20 February 2016 at http://www.eastasiaforum.org/2016/02/20/why-has-chinese-foreign-policy-become-more-assertive/ (Accessed 28 February 2017)

Michael, Martina, Mogato, Manuel, 'ASEAN breaks deadlock on South China Sea, Beijing thanks Cambodia for support', *The Livemint*, 25 July 2016 at http://www.livemint.com/Politics/OCv2k6w5ylIIzY5PCqY6mK/Asean-breaks-deadlock-on-South-China-Sea-Beijing-thanks-Cam.html (Accessed 30 October 2017)

Min Shu, 'Balancing in a hierarchical system: Pre-colonial Southeast Asia and the tribute system', *Waseda Global Forum* 8 (1), 2011

Minxin, Pei, 'Think again: Asia's rise', *Foreign Policy*, 21 June 2009 at http://foreignpolicy.com/2009/06/21/think-again-asias-rise/ (Accessed 11 June 2015)

'Modi in Singapore: PM praises Indian diaspora', *ENI*, 24 November 2015 at http://eni.news24online.com/modi-in-singapore-pm-praises-indian-diaspora/ (Accessed 18 April 2017)

Mohan, C. Raja, 'Is India an East Asian power? Explaining New Delhi's security politics in the Western Pacific', *ISAS Working Paper* no. 81, 11

August 2009 at https://www.files.ethz.ch/isn/104768/80.pdf (Accessed 17 April 2017)

______, *Modi's World*. New Delhi: Harper Collins, 2015

'More "agile fleets needed" to tackle sea challenges', *People's Daily Online*, 7 March 2017 at http://en.people.cn/n3/2017/0307/c90000-9186595.html (Accessed 7 March 2017)

Morgenthau, J. Hans, Thompson, W. Kenneth, *Politics among Nations: The struggle for power and peace* (6th ed). New York: McGraw-Hill, 1985

Moss, Trefor, 'Obama visit signals progress for Asia "Pivot"', *The Wall Street Journal*, 2 May 2014 at http://blogs.wsj.com/indonesiarealtime/2014/05/02/obama-visit-signals-progress-for-asia-pivot/ (Accessed 22 June 2015)

Mullen, D. Rani, 'India's Development Assistance: Will it change the global development finance paradigm?' April 2013 at http://www.iilj.org/newsandevents/documents/mullen.pdf (Accessed 14 October 2015)

Muni, SD, 'India's "Look East Policy": the strategic dimension', *ISAS Working Paper* no. 121, 1 February 2011 at https://www.files.ethz.ch/isn/126612/ISAS_Working_Paper_121-_Email-_India%27s_%27look-east%27_policy_the_strategic_dimension_01022011145800.pdf (Accessed 13 April 2017)

Nation branding at https://en.wikipedia.org/wiki/Nation_branding (Accessed 14 March 2017)

'New Mekong Cooperation Mechanism', *The Nation*, 19 October 2015 at http://www.nationmultimedia.com/aec/New-Mekong-cooperation-mechanism-30271164.html (Accessed 12 November 2015)

Nye, Joseph, *The Future of Power,* USA: United States by Public Affairs, 2011

Oldemeinen, Mareike, 'The Political Realism of Thucydides and Thomas Hobbes', *E-Internattional Relations Students*, 15 February, 2010 at http://www.e-ir.info/2010/02/15/the-political-realism-of-thucydides-and-thomas-hobbes/ (Accessed 16 May 2017)

Osius, Ted, 'Enhancing India-ASEAN Connectivity', *Centre for Strategic and International Studies*, June 2013 at http://csis.org/files/publication/130621_Osius_EnhancingIndiaASEAN_WEB.pdf (Accessed 15 October 2015)

'Overview: ASEAN-India dialogue relations', August 2016 at http://asean.org/storage/2012/05/Overview-ASEAN-India-as-of-19Aug16-r3fn.pdf (Accessed 30 March 2017)

Palit, Amitendu, 'Road diplomacy: How India is isolating itself in regional space', *The Financial Express*, 25 April 2017 at http://www.financialexpress.com/opinion/road-diplomacy-how-india-is-isolating-itself-in-regional-space/640908/ (Accessed 27 April 2017)

______, 'India's bid for APEC membership: Trade policy is the stumbling block', ISAS Working Paper no. 306, 26 January 2016 at https://www.isas.nus.edu.sg/ISAS%20Reports/ISAS%20Insights%20No%20%20306%20%20-%20Indias%20Bid%20for%20APEC%20Membership %20 %20Trade% 20Policy%20is%20the%20Stumbling%20Block.pdf (Accessed 17 April 2017)

______, 'India inches towards liberalisation at RCEP', *East Asia Forum*, 30 September 2016 at http://www.eastasiaforum.org/2016/09/30/india-inches-towards-liberalisation-at-rcep/ (Accessed 17 May 2017)

______, 'RCEP has to be more inclusive than TPP', *China Daily*, 23 November 2016 at http://www.chinadaily.com.cn/opinion/2016-11/23/content_27465341.htm (Accessed 9 February 2017)

______, 'India-Southeast Asia Relations: enhancing mutual benefits', *Brookings India Impact Series*, May 2015 at http://www.brookings.in/wp-content/uploads/2015/06/India-Southeast-Asia-Relations-Amitendu.pdf (Accessed 27 January 2017)

Palit, Sinha, Parama, 'China-India communication: A Doklam Dividend?' *China Policy Institute*, 10 October 2017 at https://cpianalysis.org/2017/10/10/china-india-and-communication-the-doklam-dividend/ (Accessed 31 October 2017)

______, *Analysing China's Soft Power Strategy and Comparable Indian initiatives*. New Delhi: SAGE, 2017

______, 'China's Soft Power in South Asia', *RSIS Working Paper*#200, 8 June 2010 at https://www.rsis.edu.sg/rsis-publication/idss/200-wp200-chinas-soft-power-i/#.WczNhmXBbVo (Accessed 6 July 2016)

Palitiel, Jeremy, 'China's Regionalisation Policies: Illiberal internationalism or neo-Mencian benevolence?' in Kavalski, Emilian (ed.) *China and the global politics of regionalisation*. USA: Ashgate Publishing Company, 2013

Panikkar, KM, *The future of Southeast Asia, an Indian view*. NY: Macmillan: 1943

Panos, Moundoukoutas, 'South China Sea: Beijing sends a strong message to America and Taiwan', *Forbes*, 26 December 2016 at https://www.forbes.com/sites/panosmourdoukoutas/2016/12/26/south china-sea-beijing-sends-a-strong-message-to-america-and-taiwan/#232441686042 (Accessed 14 March 2017)

Pant, V. Harsh, 'India has to do more to fix its Southeast Asian relations', *The National*, 1 October 2015 at http://www.thenational.ae/opinion/comment/india-has-to-do-more-to-fix-its-southeast-asian-relations (Accessed 1 October 2015)

Parashar, Sachin, 'India to invite heads of 10 ASEAN nations for Republic Day celebrations', *The Times of India*, 8 July 2017 at http://timesofindia.indiatimes.com/india/india-to-invite-heads-of-10-asean-nations-for-republic-day-celebtations/articleshow/59497883.cms (Accessed 9 July 2017)

Perkovich, George, 'Is India a major power?', *The Washington Quarterly* 27 (1), Winter 2003-04

Perlez, Jane, 'Rodrigo Duterte gets closer to China, and the neighbours notice,' *The New York Times*, 24 October 2016 at https://www.nytimes.com/2016/10/25/world/asia/rodrigo-duterte-philippines-china.html?_r=0 (Accessed 19 April 2017)

Pillalamarri, Akhilesh, 'Why India should "Look West" instead', *The Diplomat*, 7 March 2016 at http://thediplomat.com/2016/03/why-india-should-look-west-instead/, (Accessed 25 January 2017)

Polachek, SW, Robst, J., Chang YC, 'Liberalism and Interdependence: Extending the Trade-Conflict Model', *Journal of Peace Research* 36 (4), 1999

'President Xi's remarks on South China Sea issue', *China Daily*, 6 July 2016 at http://www.chinadaily.com.cn/world/2016-07/06/content_25989430.htm (Accessed 18 April 2017)

'President vows to bring benefits to people in realising "Chinese Dream"', *Xinhuanet*, 17 March 2013 at http://news.xinhuanet.com/english/china/2013-03/17/c_132240052.htm (Accessed 7 March 2017)

Price, Gareth, 'India's policy towards Burma', February 2013 at http://www.chathamhouse.org/sites/files/chathamhouse/public/Research/Asia/0613pp_indiaburma.pdf (Accessed 18 June 2015)

Purushothaman, Vithiyapathy, 'India's strategic dimensions in Malacca Strait', *Chennai Centre for China Studies*, 16 March 2015 at http://www.c3sindia.org/military/4901 (Accessed 17 April 2017)

Qin Yaqing, 'Why is there no Chinese International Theory' at http://ppe.wiki.hci.edu.sg/file/view/Chinese+Theory+of+IR.pdf (Accessed 28 June 2015)

Quah, Danny, 'World's center of economic gravity shifts East', *CNN*, 7 April 2011 at http://globalpublicsquare.blogs.cnn.com/2011/04/07/worlds-center-of-economic-gravity-shifts-east/ (Accessed 27 January 2017)

Raimo, Vayrynen, 'Regionalism: Old and New', *International Studies Review* 5, 2003 at http://www.wiso.uni-hamburg.de/uploads/media/11_Vaerynen_2003.pdf (Accessed 5 October 2015)

Rao, PV, Narasimha, *India and the Asia-Pacific: Forging a New Relationship*, Singapore: ISEAS, 1994

Rao, Nirupama, 'America's "Asian pivot": The view from India', 3 February 2013 at http://watson.brown.edu/southasia/news/2013/honorable-nirupama-rao-america-s-asian-pivot-view-india-full-text-available (Accessed 26 January 2017)

Ray, Trisha, 'India's Act East Policy: A track record and recommendations for the future', *Georgetown Security Studies Review*, 28 September 2016 at http://georgetownsecuritystudiesreview.org/2016/09/28/indias-act-east-policy-a-track-record-and-recommendations-for-the-future/ (Accessed 25 January 2017)

Regionalism (International Relations) at https://en.wikipedia.org/wiki/Regionalism_(international_relations) (Accessed 9 May 2017)

Reischer, Rosalind, 'India's Look East policy in the South China Sea', *The Diplomat*, 31 August 2012 at http://thediplomat.com/2012/08/indias-look-east-policy-in-the-south-china-sea/ (Accessed 29 March 2017)

Rigby, Richard, 'Tianxia', *The China Story*, 2015 at https://www.thechinastory.org/yearbooks/yearbook-2013/forum-politics-and-society/tianxia-"V‰º/ (Accessed 7 March 2017)

Rivas, Villanueva, 'Cosmopolitan Constructivism: Mapping a road to the future of Cultural and Public Diplomacy', 13 January 2010 at http://www.publicdiplomacymagazine.com/cosmopolitan-constructivism-mapping-a-road-to-the-future-of-cultural-and-public-diplomacy/ (Accessed 8 September 2017)

Roche, Elizabeth, 'India, with an eye on ASEAN, looks to deepen ties with Malaysia', *The Mint*, 8 July 2013 at http://www.livemint.com/Politics/tLPg8A3zzomuda6J71RT2H/India-with-eye-on-Asean-looks-to-deepen-ties-with-Malaysia.html (Accessed 7 May 2017)

'Rockefellers knew there was mega deposits of oil in Vietnam in the fifties' at http://www.luckinlove.com/oilinvietnam.htm (Accessed 19 June 2015)

Rosecrance, Richard, 'Regionalism and the Post-Cold War Era', *International Journal* 46, 1991

Ruggiero, Tim, 'Mill's Principle Of Intellectual Humility', *Philosophical Society.com* at http://www.philosophicalsociety.com/Archives/

Mill%27s%20Principle%20Of%20Intellectual%20Humility.htm(Accessed 16 May 2017)

Sajjanhar, Ashok, 'Taking stock of India's "Act Easy Policy"', *ORF Issue Brief*, May 2016 at http://www.orfonline.org/wp-content/uploads/2016/05/ORF_Issue_Brief_142_A_Sajjanhar.pdf (Accessed 10 May 2017)

Saran, Samir, 'Watch out China: Why the "Asian century"' might just belong to India', *The National Interest*, 2 June 2015 at http://nationalinterest.org/blog/the-buzz/watch-out-china-why-the-asian-century-might-just-belong-13025 (Accessed 13 April 2016)

Sastri, Nilkanta, *The Cholas*. University of Madras: 1975

Schelling, C. Thomas, *The Strategy of Conflict*. Cambridge: Harvard University Press, 1960/1980

Schweller, L. Randall, 'Managing the rise of Great Powers: History and Theory' in Johnston, Iain, Alastair, Ross, S. Robert (eds), *Engaging China: The management of an Emerging Power*. New York: Rutledge, 1999

Scott, David, 'India's "extended neighbourhood" concept: power projection for a rising power', *India Review* 8 (9), April-June 2009 at http://www.d-scott.com/wp-content/uploads/2013/09/india-extendedneighbourhood.pdf (Accessed 1 October 2015)

'Secretary Tillerson Meets With the Foreign Ministers of the Association of Southeast Asian Nations', *US Department of State*, 4 May 2017 at https://www.state.gov/r/pa/prs/ps/2017/05/270657.htm (Accessed 5 July 2017)

Sen, Amartya, *The Argumentative Indian*. England: Penguin Books, 2005: 79-80

Sen Gupta, Bhabani, 'India in the Twenty-First Century', *International Affairs* 73 (2), 1997

Shambaugh, David, 'China Engages Asia: Reshaping the Regional Order', *International Security* 29 (3), 2004/05

Sharma, Navrekha, 'Why Indonesia is important for India', *IDSA Issue Brief*, 20 January 2011 at http://www.idsa.in/issuebrief/WhyIndonesiaisImportanttoIndia.html (Accessed 19 June 2015)

Sharma, Yogima, 'Drones, satellites on the job as Modi pushes team to meet his election promises', *The Economic Times*, 29 April 2017 at http://economictimes.indiatimes.com/news/economy/infrastructure/government-to-quicken-pace-of-infrastructure-creation/articleshow/58425487.cms (Accessed 7 July 2017)

Shen, J, 'Duobian waijiao he duoji shijie' (Multilateral foreign relations and multipolar world), *Shijie Jingji yu zhengzhi* 10 (254)

Shimazu, Naoko, 'Diplomacy as Theatre: Staging the Bandung Conference of 1955', *Modern Asian Studies*, 48 (1), 22 July 2013 at https://www.cambridge.org/core/journals/modern-asian-studies/article/diplomacy-as-theatre-staging-the-bandung-conference-of-1955/9927713C17313F1B51167ECC4703E65B (Accessed 2 May 2017)

Sidhu, WPS, Godbole, Shruti, 'Modi's foreign policy@365: Course Action', *Brookings India*, July 2015 at http://www.brookings.in/wp-content/uploads/2015/07/Final-book.pdf (Accessed 13 February 2017)

'Singapore: US withdrawal from trade pact hurts confidence - PM Hsien Loong', *Asian Correspondent*, 1 March 2017 at https://asiancorrespondent.com/2017/03/singapore-us-withdrawal-trade-pact-hurts-confidence-pm-hsien-loong/#4WXmWS4iiczvl9jI.97 (Accessed 20 April 2017)

Singh, Abhijit, 'Why India's South China Sea stand matters', *IDSA Comment*, 19 August 2016 at http://www.idsa.in/idsacomments/why-india-south-china-sea-stand-matters_asingh_190816 (Accessed 20 April 2017)

Singh, Bhupinder, 'ASEAN's perceptions of Japan: Change and Continuity', *Asian Survey* 42 (2), 2002

Singh, Daljit, 'China's White Paper on Security Cooperation in the Asia-Pacific Region and Chinese Grand Strategy', *ISEAS Perspective*, 7 April 2017 at https://www.iseas.edu.sg/images/pdf/ISEAS_Perspective_2017_22.pdf (Accessed 18 May 2017)

Solomon, Arulraj, David, Sanyal, C. Bikas, Wildemeersch, Danny, 'Engaging with Cross-Border Higher Education in India, while sustaining the best tradition of Indian values', 2005 at https://www.oecd.org/site/imhe2006bis/37464379.pdf (Accessed 10 February 2017)

'South Asia Satellite' at https://en.wikipedia.org/wiki/South_Asia_Satellite (Accessed 8 May 2017)

'Speech by Chinese President Xi Jinping to Indonesian Parliament', *ASEAN-China Centre*, 3 October 2013 at http://www.asean-china-center.org/english/2013-10/03/c_133062675.htm (Accessed 8 May 2017)

'Speech by the Honourable Bob HAWKE AC, former Prime Minister of Australia, at the first plenary session of the 7th Xiangshan forum', *Xiangshan Forum*, 11 October 2016 at http://www.xiangshanforum.cn/

mobile/artseven/sevenforum/sspeech/fmeeting/201610/1830.html (Accessed 3 May 2017)

'Statement by India and Indonesia on maritime cooperation', *Ministry of External Affairs*, 12 December 2016 at http://mea.gov.in/bilateral-documents.htm?dtl/27806/Statement+by+India+and+Indonesia+on+Maritime+Cooperation (Accessed 17 April 2017)

Storey, Ian, *Southeast Asia and the Rise of China*. NY: Routledge, 2011

Swaine, D. Michael, 'Chinese view and commentary on Periphery Diplomacy', *China Leadership Monitor*, Summer 2014, Issue 44 at http://www.hoover.org/sites/default/files/research/docs/clm44ms.pdf (Accessed 23 February 2017)

______, 'Xi Jinping's address to the Central Conference on Work Relating to Foreign Affairs: Assessing and advancing Major - Power Diplomacy with Chinese Characteristics', 28-29 November 2014 at http://www.hoover.org/sites/default/files/clm46ms.pdf (Accessed 30 November 2015)

Tharoor, Shashi, *Pax Indica: India and the World of the 21st Century*. New Delhi: Penguin, 2012

Thayer, A. Carlyle ,*The Borderlands of Southeast Asia: Geopolitics, Terrorism, and Globalisation*. Washington: National Defense University Press, 2011

'The ASEAN Declaration (Bangkok Declaration) Bangkok', 8 August 1967 at http://www.asean.org/news/item/the-asean-declaration-bangkok-declaration (Accessed 11 October 2015)

'The Central Conference on Work relating to Foreign Affairs was held in Beijing', *Ministry of Foreign Affairs of the People's Republic of China*, 29 November 2014 at http://www.fmprc.gov.cn/mfa_eng/zxxx_662805/t1215680.shtml (Accessed 23 February 2017)

The Great Illusion at https://en.wikipedia.org/wiki/The_Great_Illusion (Accessed 14 March 2017)

'The Greater Mekong Sub-region Economic cooperation program strategic framework 2012-22', *ADB Background Paper*, August 2010 at https://www.adb.org/sites/default/files/institutional-document/32621/files/gms-sf-background-paper.pdf (Accessed 3 May 2017)

'The History of Japanese-Indian Exchange', *Ministry of Foreign Affairs in Japan* at http://www.mofa.go.jp/region/asia-paci/india/relation/relation.html (Accessed 13 October 2015)

'The Twentieth ASEAN Transport Ministers Meeting', *Joint Statement*, 27 November 2014, Myanmar at http://www.asean.org/images/pdf/

2014_upload/20%20ATM%20JMS%20Final.pdf (Accessed 15 October 2015)

Tony Tai-Ting Liu, Tung-Chieh Tsai, 'Swords in Ploughshares: China's Soft Power strategy in Southeast Asia and its challenges', *Rev. Bras. Polít. Int.* 57 (special edition), 2014 at http://www.scielo.br/pdf/rbpi/v57nspe/0034-7329-rbpi-57-spe-00028.pdf (Accessed 27 October 2015)

Tow, T. William, 'The US and Asia in 2013: From primacy to marginalisation?' *Asian Survey* 54 (1), January/February 2014

Townshend, Ashley, 'America First: US Asia policy under President Trump', *The United States Study Centre*, 16 March 2017 at https://www.ussc.edu.au/analysis/america-first-us-asia-policy-under-president-trump (Accessed 19 April 2017)

'Trump's mixed signals on S China Sea worry Asia', *TodayOnline.com*, 12 May 2017

Veeramalla, Anjaiah, 'Jokowi's global maritime axis doctrine key to Indonesia's future', *Pressreader*, 6 March 2017 at https://www.pressreader.com/indonesia/the-jakarta-post/20170306/281633895027864 (Accessed 4 July 2017)

'Vision and actions on jointly building Silk Road Economic Belt and 21st-Century Maritime Silk Road', *Ministry of Foreign Affairs*, 28 March 2015 at http://en.ndrc.gov.cn/newsrelease/201503/t20150330_669367.html (Accessed 16 May 2017)

Vogel, Ezra, 'Regionalism in Asia: Why we should stick with existing structures', *East Asia Forum*, 30 March 2010 at http://www.eastasiaforum.org/2010/03/30/regionalism-in-asia-why-we-should-stick-with-existing-structures/ (Accessed 2 May 2017)

Vuying, L, Alexander, 'How Soft Power works' at http://apcss.org/Publications/Vuving%20How%20soft%20power%20works%20APSA%202009.pdf (Accessed 11 May 2017)

Wagner, Jan-Philipp, 'The effectiveness of Soft & Hard Power in contemporary international relations', 4 May 2014 at http://www.e-ir.info/2014/05/14/the-effectiveness-of-soft-hard-power-in-contemporary-international-relations/ (Accessed 17 January 2017)

Wang F., 'Preservation, Prosperity and Power', *Journal of Contemporary China* 14 (45), 2005

Wang Yi, 'Toward a new model of major-country relations between China and the United States', *Speech at the Brookings Institution*, Washington DC, 20 September 2013 at http://www.brookings.edu/~/media/

events/2013/9/20-us-china-foreign-minister-wang-yi/wang-yi-english-prepared-remarks.pdf (Accessed 25 June 2015)

Wang Zheng, 'A new understanding of geopolitical economy', 6 October 2015 at http://blog.sciencenet.cn/blog-2211-925674.html (Accessed 2 December 2015)

Wayne M. Morrison, 'China's economic rise: History, trends, challenges, and implications for the United States', *Congressional Research Service*, 21 October 2015 at https://fas.org/sgp/crs/row/RL33534.pdf (Accessed 11 May 2017)

Weatherbee, E. Donald, *International Relations in Southeast Asia: The Struggle for autonomy*. UK: Rowman & Littlefield, 2015

'What were the causes of the Peloponnesian war?', *DailyHistroy.org* at http://dailyhistory.org/What_were_the_causes_of_the_Peloponnesian_War%3F (Accessed 4 July 2017)

White, Hugh, 'Australia extremely uneasy about US' future Asia policy', *Pressreader*, 17 February 2017 at https://www.pressreader.com/usa/global-times-us-edition/20170217/281741269178058 (Accessed 7 July 2017)

White, L. Candace, 'Brands and national image: an exploration of inverse country-of-origin effect', *Place Branding and Public Diplomacy*, 8(2), 2012 at www.palgrave-journals.com/pb/ (Accessed 9 March 2017)

White paper on China's National Defence in 2002 at https://fas.org/nuke/guide/china/doctrine/natdef2002.html (Accessed 3 May 2017)

Wroe, David, 'Hedging China: Australia joins security dialogue with US, Japan, India', *The Sunday Morning Herald*, 13 November 2017 at http://www.smh.com.au/federal-politics/political-news/hedging-china-australia-joins-security-dialogue-with-us-japan-india-20171113-gzk2qv.html (Accessed 13 November 2017)

Wu Baiyi, 'The Chinese Security Concept and its Historical Evolution', *Journal of Contemporary China* 10 (27), 2001

'Xi advocates efforts to boost China's maritime power', *Xinhuanet*, 31 July 2013 at http://news.xinhuanet.com/english/china/2013-07/31/c_132591246.htm (Accessed 29 June 2015)

'Xi Jinping attends APEC CEO Summit and delivers important speech', *Ministry of Foreign Affairs of the People's Republic of China*, 9 October 2013 at http://www.fmprc.gov.cn/mfa_eng/topics_665678/xjpfwynmlxycx21apec_665682/t1087044.shtml (Accessed 13 April 2016)

Xue Li, Xu Yanzhuo, 'The problems with China's foreign policy bureaucracy', *The Diplomat*, 17 April 2015 at http://thediplomat.com/

2015/04/the-problems-with-chinas-foreign-policy-bureaucracy/ (Accessed 22 February 2017)

Yong Deng, *China's Struggle for Status: The Realignment of International Relations*. UK: Cambridge University Press, 2008

Yong Deng, Fei-Ling Wang (eds), *China Rising: Power and motivation in Chinese foreign policy*. USA: Rowman & Littlefield Publishers, 2004

Yuan, JD, *ASEAN-China Relations*. Carlisle, PA: Strategic Studies Institute, 2006

Yun Sun, 'How the international community changed China's Asian Infrastructure Investment Bank', *The Diplomat*, 31 July 2015 at http://thediplomat.com/2015/07/how-the-international-community-changed-chinas-asian-infrastructure-investment-bank/ (Accessed 13 November 2015)

Zenn, Jacob, 'US presence evolves in Southeast Asia', *Asia Times*, 4 April 2012 at http://www.atimes.com/atimes/Southeast_Asia/ND04Ae01.html (Accessed 12 June 2015)

Zhang Feng, 'The Tianxia System: World Order in a Chinese Utopia', *China Heritage Quarterly*, January 2010 at http://www.chinaheritage quarterly.org/tien-hsia.php?searchterm=021_utopia.inc&issue=021 (Accessed 6 March 2017)

Zhang Yunling, 'OBOR: A Chinese view', *Global Asia*, 10 (3), Fall 2015

______, Tang Shiping, 'China's regional strategy' in Shambaugh, David (ed.) *Power Shift: China and Asia's new dynamics*. Berkeley: University of California Press, 2005

Zhao Hong, 'China's One Belt One Road: An overview of the debate', *ISEAS* no 6, 2016 at https://www.iseas.edu.sg/images/pdf/TRS6_16.pdf (Accessed 17 February 2017)

______, 'China's new maritime silk road: Implications and opportunities for Southeast Asia', *ISEAS* no. 3, 2015 at https://www.iseas.edu.sg/images/pdf/Trends_2015_3.pdf (Accessed 17 February 2017)

______, 'The maritime silk road and China-Southeast relations', *ISEAS Perspective*, 8 July 2015 at https://www.iseas.edu.sg/images/pdf/iseas_perspective_2015_35.pdf (Accessed 9 May 2017)

Zhu Zhenming, 'Mekong development and China's (Yunnan) participation in the Greater Mekong Sub-region cooperation', *Ritsumeikan International Affairs 8*, 2010 at http://r-cube.ritsumei.ac.jp/bitstream/10367/1183/1/30039991_8_01.pdf (Accessed 12 November 2015)

Index